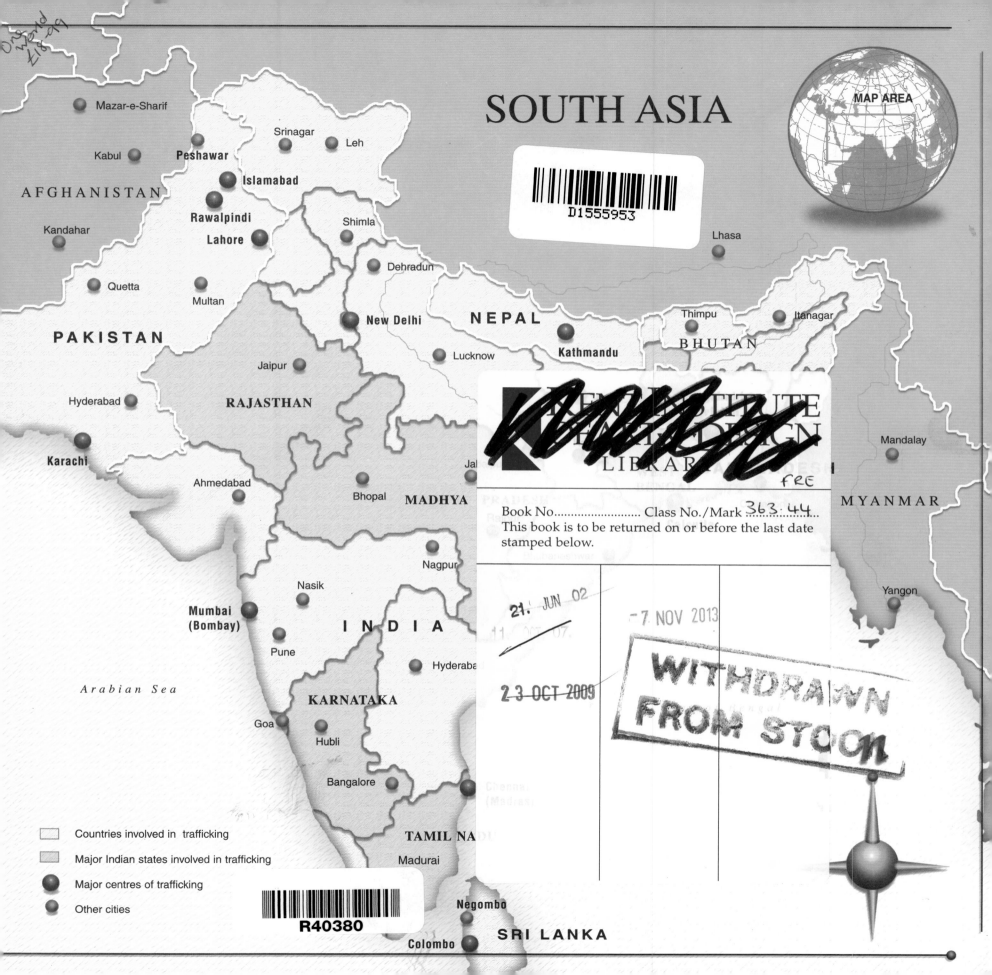

SOUTH ASIA

MAP AREA

Mazar-e-Sharif

Kabul · Srinagar · Leh

Peshawar

Islamabad

AFGHANISTAN

Kandahar · **Rawalpindi** · Shimla

Lahore · Dehradun

Quetta · **NEPAL** · Lhasa

Multan

New Delhi · Thimpu · Itanagar

PAKISTAN · BHUTAN

Lucknow · **Kathmandu**

Jaipur

Hyderabad · RAJASTHAN · Mandalay

Karachi · Ahmedabad · Bhopal · MADHYA · MYANMAR

Nagpur

Nasik · Yangon

Mumbai (Bombay) · INDIA

Pune · Hyderaba

Arabian Sea · KARNATAKA

Goa

Hubli

Bangalore · Chennai (Madras)

TAMIL NADU

Madurai

Countries involved in trafficking

Major Indian states involved in trafficking

Major centres of trafficking

Other cities

Negombo

Colombo · **SRI LANKA**

FALLEN ANGELS

THE SEX WORKERS OF SOUTH ASIA

FALLEN ANGELS
THE SEX WORKERS OF SOUTH ASIA

EDITOR
John Frederick

PHOTO EDITOR/CO-ORDINATOR
Thomas L. Kelly

FOREWORD BY Anita Roddick

Lustre Press
Roli Books

PHOTOGRAPHERS

Thomas L. Kelly   Shehzad Noorani   Anita Khemka

Mahmud   Mani Lama   Fawzan Husain

Anis Hamdani   Achinto

WRITERS

Vidhea Shrestha   Jeremy Seabrook   Munni Saha

Linnet Pike   Hasan Mujtaba   Cliff Meyers

Sunil Menon   Rajendar Menen   Harsh Mander

Anusheh Hussain   John Frederick   V. Carroll Dunham

Abha Dayal   Thérèse Blanchet

Design by Bena Sareen
Design consultancy by Kurt Meyer and Roshan Rajopadhyaya

In the text, the names of all present or former sex workers, except that of Mehrunissa and those of the Durbar Mahila Samanwaya Committee, have been changed. None of the sex workers featured in the stories, except these, appear in the photographs.

ISBN: 81-7436-100-6

© JOHN FREDERICK, 2000, on behalf of all writers.
E-mail: john@yantra.wlink.com.np
© THOMAS L. KELLY, 2000, on behalf of all photographers except Shehzad Noorani.
E-mail: tkelly@photo.wlink.com.np

363 44 FRE

Roli Books Pvt. Ltd. 2000
Lustre Press Pvt. Ltd.
M-75 GK Part II (Market), New Delhi 110 048, India
Tel: (011) 6462782, 6442271, Fax: (011) 6467185
E-mail: roli@vsnl.com, Website: Rolibooks.com

Printed and bound in Singapore

contents

Page 1: A woman of the Badi caste prepares herself for clients, while her mother and younger sister look on. *Midwestern Region, Nepal.* THOMAS L. KELLY

Pages 2–3: Early evening at the brothel door. Bangladeshi sex workers are noted in the region for their aggressive, ebullient style of solicitation. *Kandupatti Brothel, Dhaka, Bangladesh.* SHEHZAD NOORANI

Page 4: Maya, the daughter of a sex worker, doesn't go to school. She spends her days playing inside the brothel with the other children. *Kamathipura, Mumbai, India.* SHEHZAD NOORANI

Page 5: Business begins about 4 p.m. in the Mumbai brothels. Divya, Bishakha and Geetanjali prepare for the evening. *Kamathipura, Mumbai, India.* THOMAS L. KELLY

Pages 6–7: Transvestite performers make up for an evening of entertainment at a wedding party. *Peshawar, Pakistan.* THOMAS L. KELLY

Pages 8–9: Girls wait for clients in the labyrinth of narrow alleys of Kandupatti brothel district. *Dhaka, Bangladesh.* SHEHZAD NOORANI

Page 10: The daughter of a prostitute. *Dhaka, Bangladesh.* SHEHZAD NOORANI

Page 11: A bathhouse boy waits for clients. *Peshawar, Pakistan.* THOMAS L. KELLY

Pages 12–13: Evening business on Falkland Road. *Mumbai, India.* THOMAS L. KELLY

Page 14: A pregnant sex worker aggressively solicits a client. Every girl must work as far into pregnancy as possible, for she will lose most of her business until her child is born. *Kandupatti Brothel, Dhaka, Bangladesh.* SHEHZAD NOORANI

acknowledgements

Our thanks go first to the sex workers of five countries who have given us their stories, allowed us to photograph them, and shared with us their hearts, their minds and their rice.

The gates to this land were opened by many social workers, health workers, activists and mentors of the streets and villages. In addition to the 'protectors' profiled in this book—those who have been our primary sources of inspiration—we are especially grateful to Maureen Seneviratne, Bhaskar Banarjee, Dr Asha Rao, Priti Patkar, Dr Harendra de Silva, Vinod Gupta, Dr Mahendra Trivedi, Fawad Usman Khan, Kunda Dixit, H.R.S. Keertisinghe, Mahbooba Akhter Mahmood (Leena), Shireen Huq, Arun Tampoe, Shivananda Khan, Najma Sadeque, A.C. Seneviratne, Prof. Devidas Manohare, Kanak Dixit, Bishakha Datta and Dr Shilpa Merchant.

Some special people and organisations have particularly shared our concern for raising awareness of the issues surrounding sex work in South Asia. This book would never have happened without the strong support of Dick Van Blitterswijk and Rianne Knippels of the Netherlands Development Assistance Liaison Office in Kathmandu, the Government of the Netherlands, and Wendy vanden Heuvel, Gail Murphy, Jim Gollin, Michael Lemle and the Threshold Foundation. In the same breath, we would like to thank Chris Files, and Anita and Gordon Roddick of The Body Shop International (UK) for helping us get the project rolling.

A few individuals have been the yeast for conceptual fermentation, and deserve most special mention for the days and years we have spent discussing the arcana of sex work: Bob Van Grevenbroek, Meena Poudel, Dr Paul Janssen, Iqbal Hussain, Dr Ann Sturley, Ian Baker, Dr Christine Daniels, Keith Dowman, Sondra Hausner, Daniel Haber, Dr Hamid Sardar-Afkhami, Ted Worcester, Dr Michael Yorke and Kate Butcher. Reflections on this subcontinent have been enriched by comparative insights from Southeast Asia, particularly from Janchai Selanon, William Page, Jerry Hopkins and Sudarat Sereewat. The editorial side is deeply indebted, literally and figuratively, to Leland Everett and Philip Haisley, AIA, for keeping the ink flowing. And finally, bless you, Pratima Gurung, for keeping the home fires burning.

The photography side was nourished in the nascent days of this project by a handful of very caring people. In Unicef, our manifold thanks go to Urban Jonsson, Ruth Hayward, Stewart McNab, Colin Glennie (and his wife Ann), Morten Giersing and Ellen Tolmie. Thank you, Keith Leslie of Save the Children Fund (US), and thank you Kate Russell and Barend Toet of The Cover Story photo agency. Personal inspiration and assistance have come from Robert Kelly, Charles Lindsay, Mahendra Chand, Tom Cox, Pritam Mansukhani and Meena Lalwani. Mountains of gratitude go to Anuradha Koirala and Armina Lama for their kind wrath and their insight, and to Carroll Dunham, who was patient with this mad effort and put up with too many months away from home.

And last, but of course not least—or there wouldn't be a book in your hand—we thank Prarupa Mukherjee and Mitra Routh for their assistance in Calcutta, Helen Gurung for her patient photo editing and research, Sherap Sherpa for his countless hours on the scanner, and Veena Baswani for her editorial perfection in the final moments.

preface

The people in this book are real people, just as you are. If you were born into a different family, into poverty, into a South Asian village or urban ghetto, your profile might be in this book. These are stories written as they were told to us, by people whom the writers have known personally, some for many years. These are photographs that were given to us, with both generosity and purpose. 'Yes, go ahead, let people see us,' they said. 'We have nothing left to be ashamed of.'

All the photographers come from backgrounds of photo-activism. Some have spent years behind the brothel curtains. Others have arrived new to the subject, but not new to its kin—they have shot rural poverty and urban despair, the female debris of gender aggression, and the alienation of the 'untouchables'. These images come from many collective years of patience: making friends, waiting for permission and avoiding intrusion. Beatings, broken cameras and nights in jail have been part of the project.

The 14 writers bring to this project more than 100 years of experience with sex workers, as anthropologists, social workers, activists and investigative journalists. For all of us, this is our work.

We have created this book because, in a very real sense, we had no choice. Once the curtains were drawn open, once we saw 'inside', as in a nightmare we saw ourselves, our daughters, our mothers, sitting before us on the beds, waiting for clients. As we learned more, the horror in us grew. We saw the utter helplessness of the young as they entered the trade. We saw hunger for affection fighting nausea at the clients' lust. And we saw the guarded, unspoken fear of reaching even 35—the end of clients, the beginning of disease, homelessness, begging. But as we learned even more, we saw strength. We found a dignity and power we had not imagined. We laughed with them, winced at their anger, and marvelled at their concern for their children and their struggle for self-respect. We shared bottles and cigarettes and confidences. They talked frankly about us 'straights' and we found our clean world portrayed with far more reality, insight and compassion than we had ever portrayed theirs. And thus the reason for this book.

This is a small book: it's about a few people and a few basic issues that concern them. With no apologies, important pieces of this immense subject are absent. There are few numbers and statistics in this book—in the absence of adequate research, we simply don't have them. We cannot even reliably estimate the number of prostitutes among South Asia's near-billion people. Two million, four million? Nobody knows.

This is not a book of facts or a book of ethnological detail. You can find the facts in the library. This is a book of people, written and photographed from the streets. Nor is this a book replete with historical insights. Prostitution has not changed much over the millennia. Individuals and communities go into the trade today for the same reasons they did at the time of the *Mahabharata*. Cultured courtesans and temple dancers are often fielded by historians as the 'roots' of prostitution. However, these *apsaras* have as little to do with the mainstream of ancient

Jamuna, just returned home after being rescued from a brothel in Mumbai, and her sister, crying. Jamuna was abducted by a friend of her family when she was 18, and spent three years in the brothel before her rescue. *Central Region, Nepal.* THOMAS L. KELLY

sex workers as high-class call-girls with their cellular phones do with the streetwalkers of today.

This book may ruffle the feathers of a few people in the 'politics of prostitution'. It presents numerous points of view, many of them conflicting. It presents solutions to some of the 'problems', and often says why the solutions are inadequate. It addresses those in the trade by many names—sex workers, prostitutes, *beshya,* fallen angels—and doesn't have time for the diversions of political correctness. There is only one name for the people in this book: humans. It profiles only a few of the many excellent South Asian non-governmental organisations (NGOs), and will certainly add fuel to the incessant NGO in-fighting that mars interventions on behalf of sex workers and delights traffickers, pimps and the AIDS virus. And it doesn't name the donors that fund the interventions. Although it acknowledges their

A young girl shares a moment of intimacy with one of her regular clients. *Kandupatti Brothel, Dhaka, Bangladesh.* SHEHZAD NOORANI

invaluable support, the donors, unlike the problems, come and go.

Fallen Angels is a small stage, and cannot adequately present all the dramatis personae of South Asia's vast theatre of prostitution. The clients, madams, pimps and police have only walk-on parts. These few pages have not allowed much discussion of broad issues such as legislation, economics, police action, politics or media representation. Although these are important, we have tried to stay on the streets. This is a small book. We have wanted to make room for the heart, and that has taken up most of the space.

— JF AND TLK

foreword

It was provocatively pointed out to me recently that most people don't travel in search of the strange. They go to find familiarity, to experience the universal. The human condition, I believe it's called. A book on the sex trade in South Asia probably wouldn't strike many readers as the first place to look for proof of the theory, but it's here.

To read the stories and study the pictures in *Fallen Angels* is to be confronted by women, girls and boys doing what they have to do to get by with as much dignity and good humour as they can. They may well be victims of social and economic injustice, but to see them only as victims does no justice to their struggle for acknowledgement and self-respect. As John Frederick points out, 'prostitution becomes a life … maintained … by the power and the courage of the individual', however much we might wish it didn't have to be that way.

But it's always been that way. Wherever you go in the world, prostitution is looked on as the oldest profession. Equally ancient and universal is the stigma attached to people who sell themselves for sex and the reasons why they go on doing it, as *Fallen Angels* underlines so compassionately in words and pictures. The big picture—in the form of religion, politics, legal systems, corrupt police—is sketched in, but Frederick and Kelly deliberately keep the focus intimate, on life on the street. Given that attitudes differ so much from country to country within South Asia itself, given the lack of statistics or hard research into the situation, the authors

A teenage sex worker resists a man's advances. *Kandupatti Brothel, Dhaka, Bangladesh.* SHEHZAD NOORANI

have made a wise choice. This way, their players have names and faces. Many of them are the breadwinners for their families, like women all over the world. Their simple pragmatism defies sentimentalisation.

Which isn't to say that their stories aren't shocking. One cornerstone of the sex trade in South Asia is the wholesale abuse of children. In India, up to a third of all sex workers enter the profession as juveniles. In Bangladesh, they often begin at 11 and are over the hill at 16. Few things disturb us as much as the sexual exploitation of a child. Abuse of vulnerability, betrayal of trust, the destruction of innocence—all under the looming spectre of the AIDS epidemic—cut to the quick of our sense of humanity and demand action on our part. But what? The disenfranchised sell the only commodity available to them. The obvious answer is to create an environment where the options don't include prostitution. That means eradicating poverty. God knows nothing would make me happier, but reason dictates that realistically this isn't going to happen anytime soon.

So we look for other answers. Education offers hope, although *Fallen Angels* establishes all too convincingly the economic and cultural context for child prostitution. It would be so convenient to view the commercialisation of sexuality in South Asia as a side-effect of globalisation—in the same way that free trade seeks cheap labour, the sex trade uses children. But I know there is so much more to the story than that. Young Najma, for example, is a promising student in an NGO initiative, but eventually her mother forces her to enter into what amounts to the family business. That takes us back to the eradication of poverty. Still, education is a route to self-esteem, and that in turn fosters a new consciousness. The seeds of this are evident in Frederick and Kelly's book. Look at Geeta and Rajendra, defying custom and courting ostracism, sacrificing everything for their son's future as a doctor. Or the sex workers who are campaigning for decriminalisation: instead of abolishing the profession, abolish the oppression.

Their call to action acknowledges both reality and self-reliance. And in its humanity, we can perhaps eventually recognise ourselves.

— ANITA RODDICK

Nepali sex workers and a madam wait for clients in front of the 'cages' in Mumbai's working-class brothel district. Contrary to the myth of Nepali girls being coveted for their grace and beauty, they are imported to India because they are cheap. *Falkland Road, Mumbai*. THOMAS L. KELLY

1

Where Angels Fear

The Forces of Sex Work in South Asia

There may be more than two million prostitutes in South Asia—women, men, girls, boys and the 'third gender'—angels unwillingly tumbled into hell. The majority come from low-caste and tribal communities, and the remainder are cast out, fleeing abuse, supporting dependents or trafficked—for in South Asia, prostitution is not a voluntary occupation. Here, 'choice' is not an operative term. These angels have not 'fallen' because of free will or wrongdoing—they have been struck down.

South Asia shares with the rest of the world the structural disorders that send women and children into the sex industry: poverty, maldistribution of power and opportunity, urban anarchy and rural out-migration. It shares the social infirmities: gender disparity, disintegrating families, domestic violence, drugs and alcohol, indolent and absconding men, and sexual abuse.

However, the subcontinent has its own unique forms of disparity, coercion and stigma that send its marginalised into prostitution: an almost hysterical preference for male

This girl was sold to the brothel as a tsukri, *or bonded sex labourer. She went mad shortly after her arrival.* Dhaka, Bangladesh. SHEHZAD NOORANI

children, imperative virgin marriage, dowry burden, public aggression against females, and the stubborn power of *izzat,* the man's honour. Through the caste system, all are branded at birth with advantage or oppression, and through ubiquitous debt bondage, children inherit the helplessness of their parents.

Throughout India, Nepal, Pakistan, Bangladesh and Sri Lanka, there are significant variations in the venues of sex work, the official tolerance of prostitution, the genders involved, and the prevalence of children in the trade. These variations are important for the way in which each country addresses issues such as HIV/AIDS intervention, the prevention of trafficking and child prostitution, and the decriminalisation of sex work.

India embraces the full range of prostitution venues: well-established red-light districts, independent brothels, roadside truck-halts, village huts, hotels high and low, bushes, fields and back alleys. Apart from the usual police brutality, there is a high tolerance for sex workers, and they are generally free to work without public or official harassment. All three sexes, including the transgendered, ply the trade in India, and a large proportion—likely more than one third—enter the profession as children.

In the Himalayan kingdom of Nepal, sex work is furtive. There are no red-light districts, and although prostitution is common throughout the country, its existence is generally denied by the public—and by the prostitutes themselves. Few Nepali prostitutes work openly. In all urban centres, there are unnoticeable brothels on quiet streets. Most 'floating' sex workers are flitting apparitions in the back booths of tea shops or hotel restaurants, and others hide their profession behind a shop counter or vegetable stall. Almost all Nepali prostitutes are female and relatively few—for the region—are children.

In Pakistan as well, the profession is discrete. Official tolerance of prostitution is zero, and police abuse is extreme. Female prostitutes are hidden, and seldom even peak through their window curtains. Transvestite and transsexual prostitutes openly present themselves as entertainers at occasions such as wedding parties or work from their private brothels. Pakistan is distinguished for a high proportion of its prostitutes being boys and young men—perhaps higher than female prostitutes—and these work the venues usually occupied by women in India, such as the streets, restaurants and hotels.

Although Bangladesh is a Muslim country with a low official tolerance, Bangladeshi sex workers—the vast majority female—work openly, and are the most outgoing and outré in the region. The capital, Dhaka, is distinguished by its large number of street sex workers—in great part due to the government's destruction of old, established brothel districts in recent years. The brothels of Bangladesh are noted for a high prevalence of very young girl prostitutes, many of whom are bonded labourers.

Sri Lanka, like Nepal, has no designated brothel districts and a generally invisible population of female sex workers. Although very little is known about domestic prostitution in Sri Lanka, the country likely has a nearly equal number of female and male prostitutes. Male prostitutes work openly, while female prostitutes are tucked away in houses, or are ordered from the staff of hotels, bars and restaurants. Official tolerance for sex workers is high—instead, intolerance has been focused on Western sex tourists. While sex tourism by South Asian men is common throughout the region, Sri Lanka is the only country to have a significant number of prostitutes—almost entirely young males—selling sex to Westerners.

It has been said that modern South Asian prostitution is founded upon ancient Indian erotic tradition. Prostitution is hinted at in the Vedic texts, and as early as the fourth century B.C. was subject to state regulation, as prescribed in the treatise on polity, the *Artha Shastra*. A musky, romantic scent hangs over prostitution: from the erotic classic *Kama Sutra* and the sacred *devadasi* temple dancers to the courtesans of the Mughal courts and the *nauch* girls that entertained the Raj.

Little remains of the scent today, except for an expanding number of dancing-girl clubs and the film industry's obsession with the 'fallen woman' as a dramatic counterpoint to the 'virtuous woman'. Realistically, a thousand years ago the majority of prostitutes conducted their business as they do today—in flophouses, bushes and huts, for labourers, soldiers and merchants.

Women and children today enter prostitution under the same kinds of coercion that they did in the past—although the proportions were different back then. In the past, more entered as chattel from war. Raw, undisguised slavery provided a greater opportunity to freely abuse women, girls and boys, or to gift them to others. Men had more liberty to take numerous new wives and consorts, and throw away the leftovers. Caste oppression flourished,

Dipika, 23, is known as the 'Butterfly Girl' because she enjoys collecting butterflies in the fields outside Calcutta. She accompanies men to resorts to support her family and pay for her sister's education. *Bow Bazar, Calcutta, India.* ACHINTO

26

of course, and entire low-caste communities fed the sexual appetites of high-caste men.

These forms of social violence are still with us, and they, not an erotic tradition, have carved the shape of South Asian prostitution. But times have changed. What distinguishes the labourers in the modern sex industry, particularly women, is their agency. As marginalised women increasingly replace men as family breadwinners and cheap wage labourers, proportionately more enter sex work of their own unfree will—not due to enslavement but because they need to earn a buck—for sex work is often the only viable profession for women against the wall.

Some sell their bodies to feed their parents and siblings, or to pay their families' debt to the moneylender. Many of the young have been raped or have taken a boyfriend who has taken his leave. Unmarriageable, they join the ranks of the 'fallen'. For unwed mothers, sex work is often an imperative if their natal families do not take them in, for society has no place for them, and their children must eat.

Women may leave a marriage behind, fleeing violence, alcohol or abusive in-laws. Perhaps they are thrown out for a second wife because they can't bear children. They may sell their bodies while they are still married if their husbands are alcoholics or junkies, and they have children to feed. Perhaps their families are bonded labourers and providing sex for the 'masters' is part of their families' obligation.

South Asian families are becoming players in the sex industry. They are increasingly sending their daughters into prostitution as wage-earners—an economic strategy of many lower castes and tribal groups of the region, and well established in neighbouring Southeast Asia.

Hell, like heaven, has many mansions, and where women and children end up selling sex is determined by beauty, race and the manner in which they were inducted. Communities with an established tradition of sending their daughters to work often place them in better brothels, working alongside their aunts and cousins. Those forcibly trafficked are sent to the lowest stews. Women cast out by their families or husbands often end up on the street.

In patriarchal South Asia, male sex workers can usually find new employment and even marriage as they get older. But for almost all women, once in the profession there is no way out. Beyond the indelible stigma of being a 'whore', the circumstances that sent them into sex work keep them there: the absence of alternatives, the dependence of their families in the village or the children at their side, the force of the pimps and madams, and the never-ending presence of debt.

On becoming a sex worker, childhood expectations of husband and family—both the social imperative and the romantic ideal of South Asian society—are rapidly torn away. A new 'family' is found: other sex workers, madams, pimps and boyfriends. Children are borne, illness and debts are encountered, and at last, old age and loss of income are confronted. Prostitution becomes a life—an unfortunate life, but the only hand dealt by the gods. It is a life maintained by dreams, by the needs of children and parents, by the illusions of love, but most by the power and courage of the individual.

— JOHN FREDERICK

A young transvestite at a wedding party. In Pakistan, many sex workers who dress as females are transvestites, not transsexuals. While many live together in groups, others are married and support children. *Peshawar, Pakistan.* THOMAS L. KELLY

Roushan and Ayaesha are street girls. They sleep on this overbridge on English Road throughout the morning, and go out to work the streets in the evening. *Dhaka, Bangladesh.* MAHMUD

2

Slaughter of Innocents

The Prostitution of Children

Children are obtained for the back rooms of brothels from a variety of sources, none of them pleasant. Children of individual prostitutes or of ethnic sex worker communities are started early in the trade to earn money as their mothers' incomes dry up. Some bonded child labourers must pay off their debts with their bodies instead of carrying bricks or weaving mats. Children abandoned and on the street are often thankful for the protection of a brothel, if they can find one. And many are trafficked, either abducted or sold by their employers or their families.

There is no legal or social consensus in the region on the definition of a 'child'. Legally, adulthood can start as early as pubescence, as in the case of Islamic Shariah law in Pakistan. Socially, South Asian children bear Western adult responsibilities, such as child care, early in life and often marry at an age when Western children are still in their short pants. Few villagers would call a 16-year-old female a 'child'.

Whatever the numbers, a person is a child if his or her emotions and judgements have not been tempered with experience of the world. It is important to differentiate between a post-pubescent child and a pubescent or pre-pubescent child. Young children have far less ability to defend themselves against abuse, no power to negotiate

wages or condoms, and bodies more susceptible to HIV infection. And more, young children can be psychologically wounded deeper and more incurably by work in the sex trade.

Among consumers in the South Asian sex industry, Nepalis do not have a strong predilection for young children. Although child marriage is common, few sex workers start in the trade before the age of 13 or 14. Girls of this age are found along the truck routes and in the brothels of towns in Nepal's southern Tarai, along the Indian border. In the hill and mountain areas of the 'Mongolian' people, sex workers below the age of 15 are relatively rare.

Bangladesh stands out in the region for the early age at which females begin prostitution. Bonded girl children and the daughters of sex workers often begin work at 11 or 12 years of age, and 16 is over the hill. Unlike other countries of the region, there is relatively little concealment or self-censure among the clients—sex with pubescent and pre-pubescent girls is an accepted facet of the trade.

In Pakistan, while marriage of older men with young women is not frowned upon, there appears to be little market for young girl children. Young-girl-child brothels do exist throughout the country, but they are extremely covert. In the typical brothel, females usually begin to work at 14 or 15, an age at which they can almost 'pass' as a woman. Male sex workers, however, are often initiated into the trade as young as nine or 10, although 12 to 14 are considered the ages at which boys are the most 'beautiful'.

Sri Lanka has few female prostitutes under the age of 16, although, as in every country in the region, girls as young as 12 and 13 can be found working in rural areas, including the war zone. Boys are frequently sold by pimps at 10 or 11, although they don't work on their own until they are a few years older. As in Pakistan, and unlike India, male prostitution is almost by definition child prostitution—demand for a male body goes down drastically soon after pubescence.

In India, 13 or 14 are the normal ages at which a 'child of the brothel' enters prostitution, and these appear to be common ages for the initiation of trafficked Nepali and Bangladeshi girls. Among tribal communities who conduct sex work, such as the Dommara and the Bedia, girls usually start work a year or two younger. Boys often start in the profession well before pubescence, but work into adulthood.

Given the clamour about child prostitution, it is significant that almost no interventions have addressed the client—the source of the demand. The provocative word 'paedophile' is applied almost solely to pot-bellied foreigners, a negligible proportion of consumers in the region. But words have strength, and lawmakers and NGOs might be encouraged to re-tool their interventions, and the public might be shaken out of its apathy if they seriously considered that an immense number of South Asian men are indeed 'paedophiles'.

— JOHN FREDERICK

In Bangladesh, men have a taste for very young girls. A child makes up her face as her madam and an elderly client watch. *Dhaka, Bangladesh.* THOMAS L. KELLY

Boys often visit brothels in groups and use the same girl, each spending three to five minutes with her. They save money, as the girl charges little more than the rate for a single adult customer. *Daulotdia Brothel, Bangladesh.* SHEHZAD NOORANI

The Prostitution of Children

IN HER MOTHER'S FOOTSTEPS

BANGLADESH

Najma

Foreboding comments have begun to circulate about Najma.

'A pretty girl like her should not have to go to the "gate". Clients should queue at her door. This should be the busiest time of her life.'

'Najma does not listen to her mother. She does not behave well with clients.'

'She likes a boy, but this is not the time for her to get tied up.'

Born and brought up in Daulotdia brothel, a rural sex-worker community on the outskirts of Dhaka, Najma is barely 14 years old and has been engaging in prostitution for almost two years. The considerable money she earned when she first started was the object of a pride that has now vanished. Najma has lost the innocence.

At the age of eight or nine, Najma appeared remarkably astute and vivacious. She played children's games, but her talk did not fit in with my idea of childhood.

'What does AIDS look like,' Najma had asked. 'Is it like gonorrhoea or syphilis?' And she gave an astonishingly accurate description of these symptoms in a man. When she and her friends were questioned on what they would like to do when they grew up, one replied that she would work in a garment factory, another that her mother would arrange her marriage. Najma cut them short.

'Our mothers are prostitutes. Where else can we go? Of course, one day, we will have to do customers.'

Najma was already earning as an occasional dancer, performing at drinking shops. Her mother, her aunt and her elder sister were all prostitutes. She knew her life would follow the same path.

A few months after our first meeting, Najma and her friends joined an NGO school opened for prostitutes' daughters. For a while, the girls were allowed to dream of a different life. Najma learned with great facility and the NGO was especially pleased with her. When a BBC correspondent made a reportage on the school, she was selected for an interview and appeared on TV screens in England and other far-away places.

'I think now I won't have to enter my name in the police register,' she declared. 'We are taught to read and write, we are learning embroidery and the director will find us good jobs outside when we finish.'

Najma never completed the three-year course. On February 7, 1997, the day following the Muslim festival of Eid, her mother decided that the time had come for her to enter the profession. Burdened with debts, her only asset was Najma. Of course, her mother could borrow easily: her creditors knew very well that she had a beautiful daughter ready to be made into an earning 'woman'. Najma did not openly protest against her mother's decision.

'How long can a daughter hear her mother being insulted by moneylenders?' she commented.

At the beginning, Najma tried hard to please her mother and was complimented by the older women for being a good daughter—committed, hard-working and eager to earn. Ten days after her initiation, we sat in Safia Bariwalli's courtyard one afternoon and I wrote the following note. (Safia Bariwalli is Najma's *bariwalli*, madam, as well as her aunt.)

Women are busy cooking and washing clothes. Children chase each other laughing. Wearing new clothes, modest jewellery and light make-up, Najma sits with us for a while. Then, without prompting, she goes to the 'gate'. She returns soon, followed by a heavily-built, *lungi*-clad man in his forties. She leads him to her newly-decorated room, comes out to get a pitcher of water and goes back, closing the door behind her. The women carry on with their washing and, cooking, the children their play. Less than five minutes later, the *lungi*-clad man walks out, avoiding our gaze. She emerges with a bowl of water that she empties some distance away. There is a smile on her face. She has just earned 100 taka (US$ 2.25).

The aunt explains that on the first day Najma served three clients. The first one paid the auspicious sum of 401 taka, the second and the third 200 taka each. A fourth client spent the whole night with her for 500 taka. The aunt warned him to be gentle as the girl was new. Every day since she started, Najma has had three to five clients, in addition to an all-night stand. Najma is earning fast and will soon be able to repay her mother's debts. Much advice and support are extended to her. Difficult though it may be for girls Najma's age, the passage is considered normal, a stage all brothel girls necessarily experience.

'Helping a mother in crisis is a daughter's responsibility,' explained Najma, who has two elder brothers, neither of whom is asked to contribute money to the family. Her elder sister was introduced into the trade at the same age as Najma and worked as a prostitute for eight years before her mother agreed to her marriage against financial compensation by the husband. It is now Najma's turn to help.

While sitting at the gate waiting for clients, Najma keeps busy embroidering sheets with beautiful flowers and birds. She does not forget the training received at the NGO school, although its original purpose—earning an income—may have been lost. Actually, no one has bothered to check whether embroidered sheets on the bed of a prostitute increase her earnings. Since Najma left school, the NGO is not pleased with her. She is associated with the failure of a much-publicised rehabilitation programme. Najma was the first student to quit and other girls in her batch soon followed. A mother explained: 'Admiring Najma's beautiful clothes and jewellery, my daughter felt envious and asked permission to enter the trade. I agreed.'

Everyone knows that prostitutes' daughters generally enter their mothers' profession. Only the wealthiest *bariwalli* are able to marry their daughters outside with a generous dowry. Most mothers soon introduce their daughters to the trade as their own careers are short and income is needed.

Girls engaging in prostitution below the age of 18 is illegal in Bangladesh, but the law is not applied unless 'activated' by guardians, explained a magistrate. When mothers themselves request the police to authorise their daughters' entry into prostitution, the law is never activated. By acquiescing to mothers' requests—regardless of their daughters' age—the police effectively sanction mothers' rights to put daughters to work, dispose of their sexuality and terminate their childhood.

Brothel culture differs little from outside society in this respect, except that in the brothel, mothers, not fathers, are invested with parental power and authority. Arranging a daughter's marriage at the age of 12 or 13—illegal

Brothel girls dress in new clothes for the festival of Eid. In the brothels, the women are close and depend on each other for psychological support. They lend each other money if they have financial problems, to avoid borrowing from the moneylenders. *Daulotdia Brothel, Bangladesh.* SHEHZAD NOORANI

though it may be according to state law—is still considered not only legitimate and moral, but a highly meritorious act in many parts of normal Bangladesh society. This is the social context in which brothel practices must be situated. Viewed from the brothel, global references that set highly different standards—such as the UN Convention on the Rights of the Child—are remote if not unknown.

The supposed inevitability of daughters entering their mother's profession gives daughter-prostitutes a kind of legitimacy and ensures their mothers' impunity. Daughters as young as 10 or 11 years old are seen standing at the brothel gate openly soliciting clients. Some of these 'daughters' may actually be *tsukri*—bonded girls who have usually been purchased, and are deprived of the income from their work. Some are adopted daughters.

Life histories collected from 96 women in Daulotdia brothel in 1995-96 showed the average age of entry into brothel prostitution to be 13.5 years old. Daughters, adopted daughters and *tsukri* were initiated younger, at 12.5 years of age, while girls entering independently (only 16 per cent of all girls) started at 15.5 years of age.

In brothel culture, daughterhood provides a powerful ideology, adhered to by young girls in need of physical and emotional shelter, and by older women in need of status and emotional fulfillment. Fictive or not, the mother-daughter relationship creates a strong bond that may be endowed with the highest morality as well manipulated to cover the greatest exploitation. The mother-daughter tie has sacred dimensions, and raises

A sex worker, her boyfriend and their child. If they can save enough money, they say, they will settle in a house outside the brothel. *Daulotdia Brothel, Bangladesh.* SHEHZAD NOORANI

39

difficult questions about the morality of exploitation and the exploitation of morality.

In conventional Bangladesh society, however, daughters are not expected to be major providers for their natal families. They are born to be given away in marriage and bring prosperity to their husbands' lineages. There, it is said that daughters are guests in their parents' home. In the brothel, it is said that they are gold to their mothers, and mothers wish to keep them for as long as possible. Daughterhood is differently defined within two cultures, two types of economy.

There are many paths leading young girls to enter prostitution. There are daughters like Najma who enter directed by their mothers whom they want to please and are morally bound to obey. Others come from outside with a history of acute poverty, ruined reputation, failed marriages or rejection by their families. Brutal force and direct coercion sometimes commit a girl to work, but they are not considered wise methods. Rather, in the great majority of cases, girls are already made vulnerable by a society particularly harsh to them, and are easily enticed into prostitution. A few quite knowingly 'choose' the profession.

Prior to 1995, Bangladesh NGOs had ignored brothels. The threat of AIDS and the money released by donors for controlling the global pandemic rapidly changed the situation. A new territory was discovered and partitioned among contenders. Intervention projects were quickly set up and 'experts' mushroomed overnight. Unfortunately, in their haste, NGOs behaved like most discoverers. They did not bother to explore

In a rural brothel community surrounded by rice fields, a madam and girl wait for clients 'at the gate'. *Daulotdia Brothel, Bangladesh.* SHEHZAD NOORANI

the previous chapters of this age-old institution. Like well-intentioned missionaries, they came to teach, diagnose, treat and rehabilitate, expecting rapid results.

Following its failure to rehabilitate Najma and her friends, the NGO in Daulotdia is rethinking its approach. Perhaps girls ought to be cut off from their mothers and the environment in which they live, they reason. They have plans to erect more buildings and delineate a 'clean' space for daughters. The problem is that institutions aiming to separate the pure from the impure inevitably gather a heap of garbage at the back door. I borrow the concept of garbage from 92-year-old Anontho, the oldest woman I met in the brothel.

'When I entered the brothel in the 1920s,' she said, 'they called us *beshya, nauti*. Now they call us "bad women". Before, there were two societies. We were left in peace. No one came to burn down our quarters and beat us up (as happened in Goalondo-Daulotdia in the mid-1980s). Now, there is only one society. It's yours, and we are your society's garbage.'

The rehabilitation of the many Najmas in Bangladesh will certainly not be achieved through embroidery classes, nor through the removal of daughters from their mothers' corrupt surroundings. Najma is part of a system. Her prostitution is a business involving a long chain of actors and actresses. Her mother, her aunt, her unemployed brothers, her mother's moneylenders and everyone else benefiting from the brothel economy—including the police, her forty-year-old client, and respectable society that needs prostitutes to create its own purity—all prostitute Najma.

BY THÉRÈSE BLANCHET
PHOTOGRAPHS BY SHEHZAD NOORANI

CARING FOR THE CHILDREN OF THE BROTHELS

Mehrunissa Shah

Bhandup, two hours south of Mumbai, is a raw industrial suburb nestled incongruously in a cradle of arid, brown hills. Its red-light district is a maze of small lanes and open sewers winding among shanty houses, hanging laundry and banyan trees wrapped in tinsel garlands. Mehrunissa approaches, her head covered, dressed in a green sari. Even from a distance, she radiates dignity and immense strength. Thirty-two years ago, Mehrunissa was taken from her mountain village in Nepal. She has never returned.

'I had just turned 14. One morning I woke up early and walked downstairs. The fire was burning, and my father's friend was sitting on a mat talking with my parents. They were talking about me. My father told me I was going to be given a wonderful opportunity. "You have a job in the city," he said. "There is a rich white *memsahib* there. You will work for her, care for her children. You will earn good money." How could I know what that meant?

Mehrunissa Shah entered the brothels of Mumbai when she was fourteen. Now 46, she operates a crèche for the children of prostitutes. Mehrunissa has inspired sex workers and social workers throughout India to create organisations for the protection of brothel children. *Bhandup, Maharashtra, India.* THOMAS L. KELLY

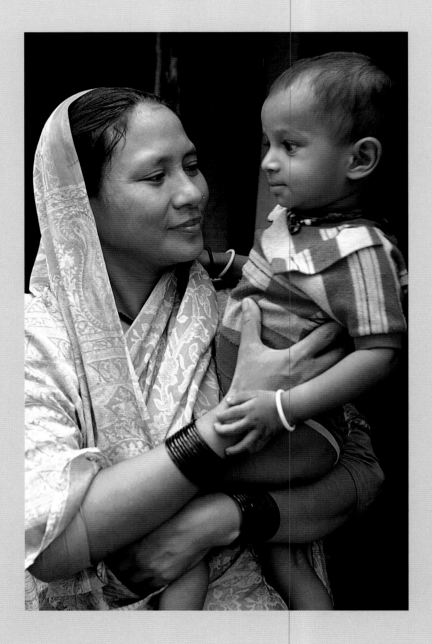

'A few days later, I travelled with my father's friend to Mumbai. We arrived at a big house and I was left with a Nepali lady. "Where is the *memsahib*, where are the children?" I asked. She replied, "What *memsahib*? You are a *randi*, a prostitute. You will earn your living selling your body." After some days, after I cried, I gave in. What could I do?'

Mehrunissa had been working for four years in the same brothel when a man named Moustaffa started seeing her. 'He never touched me. He paid more than my price just to spend time talking with me. I fell in love with him, even though I knew he was married and had children.'

After a few months, the madam trusted him enough to let them go out together. 'One day, he took me to the beach and thrust a bundle of money in my hands. "Take this," he said. "Go home, leave this hell." I started to cry. I'd hoped he would marry me and take me away. I said to him, "I can't go. I can't even find my way back to the brothel. Where can I go? I can never return to my home. I have to stay."

'Moustaffa had to leave town for three months. During that time, a Marwari man approached my madam and paid her a large sum of money to buy me. I became his common-law wife, even though he was already married. I didn't care. I was out of the brothel and I wanted a child. I had to have one person I could call my own. I never saw Moustaffa again.

'The Marwari man was a good-for-nothing, and quickly began losing his business and property. Before he lost it all, I persuaded him to start up a brothel here in Bhandup. I managed seven girls. Eventually his family took him back. I was relieved.

'I now had a son, and with my business, I had enough money to support him. But I looked at the girls around me. I knew what they felt for their children, I knew they were helpless to take care of them. So I started this crèche. I gave up my brothel about six years ago.'

Mehrunissa sits with the dignity of a goddess on the floor of her home, a two-room, windowless tin shack that doubles as a crèche for the children of prostitutes and poor working women. Babies swing in hammocks suspended from the rafters, two tiny girls giggle in the corner, and a little boy pulls at the hem of Mehrunissa's sari. A rusty fan stirs the hot, humid air, and a Hindi film song blares from a small transistor radio.

For 12 years, Mehrunissa has cared for the children of the Bhandup red-light district in this squatter's hut. Although she refuses publicity and rarely leaves her community, her name is known among the brothels of western India, and she has inspired the growth of crèches for prostitutes' children as far away as Calcutta and Madras.

'Now I have this crèche, and I care for the children while their mothers work. I want a better life for them, a life of love and care.

'You know, sometimes I think my father knew what was going to happen to me. Twenty years after I had been sold, he came down here to find me. He pleaded with me to come home and care for him in his old age. He offered me family land. I said, "Father, I've been a prostitute and a brothel-keeper for 20 years. What can you give me now? If you can give me back my dignity, I will return."'

—Vidhea Shrestha

43

NOWHERE TO HIDE

Tariq

Tariq was 12 years old when he ran away from home. The son of a gatekeeper and the eldest of four children, he left Peshawar because he 'just wasn't happy'. With a few pieces of clothing and 900 rupees stolen from his father, he embarked on a journey that he thought would result in a better life.

Travelling south into Punjab, Tariq arrived at one of the country's largest bus stands, and one of its most notorious—for drugs, alcohol, gambling, smuggled goods, thefts, occasional bomb blasts, regular murders and the unforgivable 'sin' of men having sex with boys.

The bus stand spreads over nearly 9,000 square metres—an immense hive of buses, workshops, hotels and thousands of people, arriving or leaving for their destinations. Approximately 40,000 people are said to pass through every day. Mechanics, black with grease, shout for their tools from under the buses. In the restaurants, *chaiwallas* (tea sellers) pour steaming hot tea for the customers who sit smoking and watching provocative dances and movies on video, while little waiter boys lurk around the tables to get a glance. Inside the myriad small hotels, the innkeepers, called *maaliks,* sit waiting for their customers.

Tariq began work almost immediately as a bus cleaner, earning three or four rupees for cleaning a bus. At night,

Young boys, many of whom are Afghan refugees, clean buses and perform other services for the drivers, who take them on as 'assistants'. Some of the boys complain of sexual harassment. *Rawalpindi, Pakistan.* THOMAS L. KELLY

he slept on the floor of a local canteen. This routine went on for a couple of months, until Tariq was approached by the *maalik* of a hotel in the bus stand.

'He told me that he would employ me for sweeping his hotel. The money was good, so I agreed.'

Not only was the money much better than what he'd been earning, but the *maalik* offered him free board and lodging. He accepted. A month later, the *maalik* asked Tariq to prostitute himself to the hotel clients.

'First I said that I am not going to do this *ganda kaam,* dirty work. But then *pakri pakri ho gayee,* they caught me.'

When asked to explain what he meant, Tariq said, 'The hotel owners get you arrested by the police. They pay the police 200 rupees (US$ 5) to arrest us and then they tell us that they have paid 2,000 rupees for our bail. Then they put a loan on us.'

Tariq was subsequently asked by the *maalik* to pay back his 'loan' not in cash, but in labour. Thus Tariq's life as a sex worker began. Today, he has been in the trade for five years.

According to the boys, the police are the most corrupt and powerful part of the prostitution nexus. Police constables themselves admit that they get a regular cut from raids on inns and hotels, as well as smuggling, theft and the narcotics trade. Though the police are heavily involved in the prostitution trade, sometimes orders from their higher-ups force them to conduct raids in the area. Most of the hotel *maaliks* are informed well in advance so that they can protect themselves, and the police can make some money.

Boy sex workers say that some of the police are hand in glove with the hotel *maaliks* and pimps. It is always the boys who are arrested: they are the lowest rung of the ladder and do not have any real control. The police extort the boys' earnings or book them under the Vagabondary Act, a minor bailable offense. When a policeman was asked what they do with the boys once they arrest them, he said 'Depends on his owner. If he has no backing, we send him to jail.'

Tariq has sex with four or five clients a day. He says that they prefer boys who are 'fair-skinned, pretty and babyish'. A boy prostitute's greatest asset is his 'beauty'—that is, the more he looks like a girl: light-skinned, slim, with a 'soft' (read hairless) body. The pimps and *maaliks* encourage the boys to look 'attractive and feminine'. The construct of masculinity in this society advocates a heterosexual preference and identification; sexual relationships with 'men' are taboo. A man who has sex with a male prostitute looks for familiar symbols to associate with and possibly reduce his own cognitive dissonance and self-imposed fear of censure. The preference for effeminate boy prostitutes could stem from this.

At the bus stand, Tariq's clientele consists mainly of soldiers, but there are also travellers in transit, local policemen and elderly men. The *maalik* has sex with Tariq as well, but 'he does it for free,' Tariq says. The policemen are also not charged for sex, but they usually leave him a tip of 20 or 30 rupees. According to Tariq, the *maalik* takes 200 to 300 rupees from each client but gives him only 50. If the boy gets a client himself, he is allowed to keep all the money. Tariq is sometimes permitted to refuse a client, but he normally doesn't for fear that the *maalik* will try to recover his loan from him.

Tariq says that the maximum time he spends with a client is 10 to 15 minutes. Clients use spit as a lubricant to ease intercourse, and after a short while it is all over. Tariq's experience of sex has been anal intercourse and little else, with the client nearly always being the active partner. Myths and cultural superstitions around masturbation prevent most of the clients from seeking it and the boys from indulging in it. Masturbation is commonly thought to create 'weakness' in a man, may even render him impotent, and could cause diseases such as gonorrhoea. Tariq says that some clients like to kiss, but that is seldom. Anyway, in his opinion: 'The clients who want foreplay are no better than those who don't. I just tune off when they're having sex with me.'

Tariq smokes hashish regularly. Alcohol, snuff and hashish are routinely used by most of the boy prostitutes of the bus stand. Those who have access to heroin smoke it occasionally. These drugs are not difficult to come by, and pimps, clients or *maaliks* often give them to the boys. Tariq's *maalik* provides him with hashish most of the time. He says hashish makes him feel 'peaceful' and helps him shut out emotions which he has no space to express. Most of the boys agree that drugs such as hashish numb the pain of anal intercourse and the feelings of depression which almost always follow the act.

Sex with multiple partners and lack of education about protection leave Tariq vulnerable to all kinds of STDs (sexually transmitted diseases), including HIV/AIDS. His only awareness of condoms is that they are 'used when one has sex with women to avoid pregnancy'. The boys' knowledge of STDs and AIDS is scant, and most suffer from STDs. They see AIDS as another STD for which a cure is not available—and vaguely report its symptoms as 'blood in the urine' or 'a disease that eats you up from the inside'. Tariq says that he feels he is in no danger from AIDS as 'it only happens to dirty boys and I bathe every day, sometimes even twice a day'.

Markets, bus terminals and other congested public spaces are venues for boy sex workers in Pakistan. Many, such as this boy, who sell watches on the street are sex workers. *Rawalpindi, Pakistan.* THOMAS L. KELLY

Tariq is fed up with the work he does and he misses home, especially his mother. 'I cry when I miss her a lot.' He has thought about leaving this work hundreds of times, but fear holds him back. 'There were two boys who ran away from here and their *maalik* followed them to their houses. He told their parents that they did bad work at the bus stand.' If his *maalik* were to do this, Tariq has no

doubt that his father would kill him. His other fear is that if he leaves without paying back his loan, the *maalik* would kill him himself.

The boys realise that they can never return home to their families. Their work is a source of shame and guilt because it violates the religious and cultural code under which they have been raised. 'In the light of the *Quran*

and *Sunnah*, this is *haraam* (unclean) and God destroyed a whole nation to punish them for their acts.' Ironically, this is also the only belief that unites the residents of the area—the boys who sell sex, the pimps, the *maaliks* and even the clients.

The boys understand that it is only here, around the bus stand, that they are not reviled for what they do, at least amongst their peer group. This place of so much pain is also the only place where they can find acceptance. Like being a victim of domestic violence, a divorcee, or coming from a 'broken home', the shame and ignominy they would face in the 'outside world' is too great a price to pay. Being caught in such a situation probably infuses a certain degree of helplessness and fatalism, which is why their plans for the future seem extremely bleak. Tariq has wanted to leave the trade for five years, but he is still unable to do so.

BY ANUSHEH HUSSAIN
PHOTOGRAPHS BY THOMAS L. KELLY

Street children relax, smoke and watch mildly pornographic videos in a restaurant of a large bus terminal. Boys such as these are often coerced into prostitution. *Rawalpindi, Pakistan.*
THOMAS L. KELLY

TEACHING THE BOYS HARD SKILLS
The Don Bosco Technical Centre

In the seaside tourist village of Negombo, Sri Lanka, it's easy to find a child. They ride by on their bicycles propositioning single male tourists, and their pimps stroll the beaches or lounge outside the bars. Many of the charming, quiet guest houses provide room service. Beneath the soft beauty and friendly atmosphere of Negombo, something smells.

Inland a few blocks, down a lane through the coconut trees, a group of clunky institutional buildings spreads out over a wide, threadbare compound. It's not an unpleasant place, but plain, functional. Here, the unsettling feeling of the lovely resort town is dispelled. There's a feeling of protection—a little severe, but caring.

The Don Bosco Technical Centre, a branch of the Don Bosco Salacian Society, is run by Father Anthony Pinto, a quick-talking, impatient man in a white cassock. If you haven't anything to contribute, he doesn't have the time. He has other work to do, such as taking care of several hundred boys from seven to 17—boys from broken families and trashed environments, many of whom are former prostitutes for foreign tourists.

In the 11 years since Father Pinto started this rehabilitation centre, throwing cows out of a cowshed to make room for the first boys, he has put more than 350 back on their feet—self-confident, well-trained, and solidly employed in the real world.

Many of the boys are from poor, tough fishermen families. 'Our outreach workers contact them on the beach, sometimes in their houses,' says Father Pinto. 'Sometimes the workers get chased out, or the parents beat them up.'

Counseling, formal education and especially job training are central to Father Pinto's rehabilitation strategy. 'When they are about 16, we teach them hard, useful skills.' The Don Bosco Technical Centre teaches electronics, carpentry, refrigeration, printing, auto mechanics and computer technology, as well as boat mechanics for the sons of the fishermen.

'Our boys are easy to place because they are well trained. Now they're working instead of selling their bodies. A boy who is selling his body is maybe making 30,000 rupees (US$ 440) a month, but that money doesn't remain in his hand. After he finishes rehabilitation, we find him a job. Maybe he starts with a salary of 3,000 rupees, but that money remains in his hand.'

Most of the centre's graduates are now married and settled down. Some come back to speak to the boys in the school, to tell them that there's a chance. Still, when they first come off the beaches, few boy children think there's a chance for anything except more hell.

'The boys who've been abused, they have lost their confidence. They have been mentally shattered. It's a big scar that cannot be wiped out. Rehabilitation, to build up their lives again, takes so much time and energy.'

—JF

A European man, well known to the police as a paedophile, waits in a schoolyard to meet a child sex worker. The meeting was arranged by the boy's pimp. *Negombo, Sri Lanka*. THOMAS L. KELLY

3

Export Commodities

Trafficking on the Subcontinent

'Trafficking' is a loaded word, encompassing a large, diverse set of phenomena. In general parlance, 'trafficking' implies movement across national borders—although it is abundantly clear that the vast majority of trafficked persons in South Asia are trafficked within their own countries. Distinguishing between 'in-country' and 'cross-border' trafficking is imperative if laws and interventions affecting the majority of trafficked persons are to be effective.

'Trafficking' also implies the presence of an outside agent who abducts a person into prostitution by force, promise of reputable employment, fake marriage or other deceit. Thus, persons who are sold into prostitution by their husbands or employers, or are sent off as wage-earners by their families have been ignored in South Asia until very recently. Today, the definition of trafficking is being tightened with the adjuncts 'coercive' versus 'family-based' or 'hard' versus 'soft'.

Little is known of the proportion of sex workers who have been trafficked, as few will readily admit that they 'chose' to enter prostitution. Of the countries in the

region, Nepal appears to have by far the lowest proportion of trafficked sex workers. There is not a large demand for young children, who are by definition trafficked, by whatever means, and there are no large cities that can hide brothels of 'unwilling' sex workers. Nepal is, however, a well-known supplier for the Indian sex industry, and has been for many years. Since family-based trafficking is well established in a only few districts, the large number of Nepalis in Indian brothels suggests that coercive trafficking has a substantial impact in much of the country.

Sri Lanka has little in-country trafficking, although there are numerous, but generally unreliable, reports of boys being trafficked from poor or war-damaged parts of the country down to the beach resorts to serve foreign sex tourists. From Sri Lanka, however, a large number of adult women travel to the Gulf States, primarily with the intention of working as domestic labourers. Since little research has been conducted in the destination countries, how many of these end up in sex work is not known.

Bangladesh has a high level of in-country trafficking of females. In part, this is due to the prevalence of child bonded sex labourers, called *tsukri,* and to the large client demand for young children. Bangladeshi families are still reluctant to use their girl children as wage-earners, so it is likely that the prevalent mode of trafficking is coercive. Bangladesh is a supplier of many females, and some boys,

In Bangladesh, a large proportion of girls are either trafficked into the brothels or enter as *tsukri* (bonded sex labourers). *Tanbazar Brothel, Narayanganj, Bangladesh.* SHEHZAD NOORANI

to the trade in India and Pakistan, and a large, but unknown number have been sent to the Gulf States.

India is not a major exporter or importer of trafficked persons, although, to fill its own vast needs, in-country trafficking is ubiquitous. Given the marriage imperative and the burden of dowry on the poor, much of the trafficking is by men who concoct hasty, fake marriages. Family-based trafficking occurs with many small-caste and tribal groups who have a tradition of female wage-earning through sex work. In some parts of the country, religion provides a cover for family-based trafficking—families may receive a 'gift' from an agent when they 'marry off' their daughters to a deity, and may then receive regular income from her sex work.

Except for some women sent to the Gulf States, Pakistan is not a major supplier, although it is a receiving country for many Bangladeshi women as well as some Afghan refugee women and boys. In-country trafficking is considerable, however, and trafficked women may make up a high proportion of those in prostitution in both rural and urban areas. Abduction of bonded women and children, kidnapping, fake marriages and the sale of extra wives into prostitution appear to take precedence over family-based trafficking.

Client demand, especially for children, will keep the business growing unless—and quite as unfortunately—increased 'voluntary' entry of marginalised girls and women can fill that demand. A not unlikely scenario is that South Asia will follow the rest of the developing world—more families will discover that the sale of their daughters' bodies can buy the rice, and families will replace coercive traffickers as the agents that send South Asian women and children into prostitution.

— JOHN FREDERICK

The three women on the left were arrested in 1999 for the alleged trafficking of Nepali girls to Mumbai. *Hanuman Dhoka Jail, Kathmandu, Nepal.* THOMAS L. KELLY

Nepali village girls, such as these, are potential victims of trafficking. In many rural communities surrounding the capital city of Kathmandu, families have been sending their children to Indian brothels for several generations. *Sindhupalchowk District, Nepal.*
THOMAS L. KELLY

Trafficking on the Subcontinent

IN THE FAMILY BUSINESS

NEPAL and INDIA

Meena

NEPAL

In Chautara, a Tamang village north of the Kathmandu Valley, Bhim Tamang is a relatively wealthy man. His cottage is roofed with tin, and his son's motorcycle is parked outside, next to the buffalo shed. Although he has no electricity, a television stands in the corner of the room, covered with cloth.

'We will have electricity here in a few months,' he says.

Bhim's prosperity is a result of his fortune to have fathered four daughters. Three are working in the brothels of Mumbai. The fourth, age 12, will go next year.

'Gurung and Magar families send their sons to the army. Their sons send money home. Why shouldn't we send our daughters to help us?'

Bhim's sister-in-law concurs. 'Look at Kamala, our neighbour. She went to Mumbai years ago. She helped her family. Now she's returned: she's brought gold, she paid for a water system for the houses on our hill. We are poor people here. We can't grow enough food; the government doesn't help us. We must depend on our daughters and sisters.'

Each year, thousands of women and girls migrate from Nepal to work in the brothels of India. Some are abducted, some are duped into marriage and sold, others go to support their families. On one hillside in Nepal, a visiting journalist recently calculated that five 'impoverished' villages receive an annual income of 2.5 million rupees (US$ 37,000) from the earnings of their women and girls in Mumbai. While an increasing number of girls are from urban areas, the majority still come from rural villages scattered throughout the country.

INDIA

Unlike the other girls in her brothel, Meena keeps her hair short. She paints each fingernail of her left hand with polish of a different colour, and keeps her collection of 'imported' nail polish bottles locked in a trunk in the back room where she entertains. On rare occasions, if she likes a client and he has the money to spend for her time, she brings out her bottles to show him.

'You're a modern girl,' they sometimes say. Many clients don't like 'modern girls', especially those who swear and smoke too many of their cigarettes, as Meena does. Most of the clients like Meena, however, so her madam Sobha puts up with her. As for Meena, she doesn't likely give a damn.

Meena is 19 and works in a small 'welcome' brothel off Shuklaji Road, in the centre of Kamathipura, Mumbai's largest red-light district.

'When I was a child, I knew I would end up here. My aunt and my older sister were in Mumbai. When I was maybe nine, I remember Sobha coming to my village to take girls away. Some Tamang girls in Kamathipura have been brought by force. But not so many. Many are like me.'

NEPAL

Until the last decade, the majority of girl trafficking from Nepal to India was confined to several districts surrounding the Kathmandu Valley and small areas along the Indian border. Most Nepali females in the brothels of Mumbai were from the Tamang ethnic group. Today, the ethnic and regional composition of working women and girls is changing. Field observers have noticed a much wider range of Nepali ethnicities in Indian brothel districts.

The export of girls from Nepal is not a new phenomenon: its methods have been proven and some participants have been involved in the business since it took its modern form approximately 35 years ago.

In the early 1960s, Indian cities entered the post-Independence phase of modernisation and urban expansion. This period roughly coincided with the advent of South Asia's cold war. In response to a perceived threat from China, India militarised its northern borders, building roads to provide access. *Tekhadars,* or labour agents, drew many Nepali labourers out of the hills. They also recruited women, the majority, Tamang, Rai and Limbu, to service the labourers and the army. When India's urban expansion began, the *tekhadars* modified their strategies to fill the needs of the village men working in the cities. Thus began Nepal's most lucrative export industry: the shipment of its girls to India.

Divya entered the Indian brothels from Nepal many years ago. Today, Mumbai is her home. She has lost much of her spoken Nepali and has no desire to return to her native country. *Kamathipura, Mumbai.* THOMAS L. KELLY

Today, trafficking is an established business in the Tamang districts of Sindhupalchowk, Nuwakot and Kabre Palanchowk. Although the Nepal government, the media and most Nepali NGOs still characterise all traffickers as villains who steal the innocent from the hills through guile or force, in these districts most of the 'traffickers' are merely village men, women and boys. They are frequently amateurs, acting as middlemen or as 'mules' to transport the girls to India. They often enter trafficking for the same reasons that families sell their girls—to escape a dead-end life of work and poverty. They willingly give up lives of hard labour and enter the sex trade, transporting a girl now and then for easy living, motorcycles and televisions.

In many villages whose girls are regularly sent to the brothels, there is a 'matchmaker', a village resident who acts as an intermediary for the buyer in India. Often a woman, the matchmaker's job is to seek out a girl with beauty and youth—one for whom the brothel owner will pay a good price—and convince the family to sell her. She visits the girl's home to soften the family's fears, describing the good life their daughter will have and the wealth she will send home.

Poverty lowers the resistance of village people to the entry of their daughters into sex work. In the impacted district of Sindhupalchowk, only five per cent of the land is fit for cultivation and excessive population has strained all resources—cultivable land, water and firewood. Farm work is seasonal, and men and boys earn extra income from portering, if work is available. The pressures of poverty fall heavy upon the children, and heaviest upon the girls.

Village employment cannot match the wealth offered by the sex industry. This, more than any other

59

factor, frustrates preventive programmes. A family can sell their daughter for more money than they could make in five years, and can often expect a regular income from her labour. When they are hungry, it is difficult to resist.

Their resistance is further lowered when they see the wealth of those around them—other villagers who have profited from the sale of their girls. In the high-transportation areas, many of the houses have new tin roofs and plate glass windows; inside are new pressure cookers, radios and cassette players. The comparative prosperity of their neighbours, coupled with tales of girls' success in India, easily convince villagers to send their daughters away.

Today, the majority of NGO interventions, supported by bags of donor funds, are directed at the few 'danger districts' surrounding the Kathmandu Valley. These interventions are designed on the premise that the girls are duped or forcibly abducted into prostitution, and that their families are passive innocents. Until very recently, NGOs and donors have ignored the obvious: that the 'danger districts' cannot possibly supply the vast number of Nepali females that fill the brothels of India, and that villagers whose girls and women have worked in Indian brothels for 30 years are not likely to be terribly naïve about what is going on.

INDIA

Sita and Meena are friends, each other's only friend in the brothel. Although Meena will talk or quarrel with anyone, Sita almost never speaks, even to Sobha or her own clients. Sobha doesn't appreciate Sita's sullenness and would move her on except that Sita is so beautiful and the clients keep coming back.

'She's a Brahmin,' confides Meena. 'From western Nepal. Hah!'

Meena finds it entertaining that a high-caste girl is working here among her fellow 'Mongolians', her word for the hill people.

'Her family married her to some Brahmin guy when she was a kid. Right away, the guy is playing around. After a year he brings home a second wife, the *mujee* (asshole). So Sita went back home. She had a hard time. Somehow she ended up here, I don't know how.'

Likely, Sita fits the stereotypical profile of the 'trafficked girl': a fall out from a bad marriage; lovely, perhaps not too intelligent; from a poor, perhaps uncaring family. Brothel fodder—the kind of girl whom traffickers are looking for. Probably her family didn't sell her because she doesn't send money home, and nobody comes from Nepal to collect her earnings. She is alone.

Meena is not alone. A few months ago, her older brother showed up at the door. 'With his hand out,' Meena says. She gave him some money and packed him off. 'My parents need money, not this *mujee*. He'll spend it all on jeans and girls before he gets back to Nepal,' she laughs.

Sita the Brahmin is the new type of Nepali girl in the brothels of India. Today, girls from far beyond the Tamang community end up in Mumbai. For the most part, it appears unlikely that their families have sold them. Often they come of their own accord, fleeing an abusive husband and in-laws, or seeking an alternative to village labour. Many have been ostracised by caste or by having illegitimate children, and have decided that if society has

A sex worker solicits a client. *Falkland Road, Mumbai.*
SHEHZAD NOORANI

60

dumped them, they may as well make money in Mumbai rather than give free sex to police and punks in their home village.

Some are victims not of their families or of social ostracism, but of the sexual slave trade—girls stolen from villages, carpet factories and streets and sold for cash. Those who resist their new owners' demands are often beaten into sexual submission, locked in their brothels, and denied almost everything, including condoms.

Perhaps Sita is different, because Sobha does not run a brothel of trafficked girls. She doesn't own them; she just hires them, usually against a lump sum 'advanced' to the family. Although the girls must work until they repay their debts, the madam is wealthy and has no need to keep her girls in servitude. This is a 'welcome' brothel, not 'the cages', she would say, referring to the hell-holes round the corner, frequented by working-class men.

'I'm lucky,' says Meena. 'Sobha is a nice woman, better than most of those bitches. My sister worked here before, so when I came here five years ago, I didn't have a very difficult time. The first few months, Sobha only sent me a couple of clients a night. She let me and Sita go out, and we went to so many movies.' Meena rattles on about the latest Hindi film stars. 'She gave me nail polish. I like nail polish.'

Most of the clients who come to Sobha's brothel are businessmen, students or government employees. Condoms are required—unless the man is rich.

'One woman here, an older woman, got sick with AIDS recently,' says Meena. 'They sent her away. Now all of us are a little scared. We try to convince the men to use condoms, but it doesn't always work. Sometimes they're drunk and they force us to have sex before Sobha can come and throw them out. Sometimes the men are wealthy, and Sobha tells us not to make a fuss if they don't want to use condoms.'

Meena sits cross-legged on the couch, fussing with her nails, looking at the television, ignoring the waiting clients.

'No, I don't like working here. I hate it. But I do it for my family. I won't go home to the village. Go home and do what? Maybe I'll go back and live in Kathmandu, start a beauty parlour. I can't yet, I haven't saved enough money. How can I go back with no money?

'I'm afraid I'm going to get sick one day. I don't like to think about it. I like to think about having children and having my own home. But this is just thinking, isn't it?'

BY JOHN FREDERICK
PHOTOGRAPHS BY THOMAS L. KELLY
AND SHEHZAD NOORANI

Alleged trafficker Rajan (centre) is booked on evidence from Jamuna (left) and Jyoti (right). Jamuna spent three years in the brothels of Mumbai, before being rescued in 1998. Rajan had earlier trafficked Jyoti's sister, and later sold Jyoti to the same brothel. *Hanuman Dhoka Jail, Kathmandu, Nepal.* THOMAS L. KELLY

PROTECTION FOR THROW-AWAY CHILDREN
Maiti Nepal

Anuradha Koirala, a 49-year-old former school teacher, is the champion of the most defenseless in Nepali society: children who are trafficked from their villages to the brothels of Mumbai. Six years ago, Anuradha started a small shelter for 'girls at risk': abandoned babies, rape victims, girls without families, street children, those for whom prostitution was often the only way to survive.

'These are throw-away children,' says Anuradha. 'All children need a *maiti*, a mother's house, and that is what I give them.' And thus Maiti Nepal was born.

Confined to the shelter under strict supervision, the older girls are put in charge of the infants, cooking and cleaning, learning to read and write in their spare time. At first, Anuradha was criticised for her imperious style, but she quickly drew round her a dedicated following of social workers, students and teachers.

Within a few years, the rapid growth of child trafficking shocked the tiny Himalayan nation. While other social workers were wringing their hands, Anuradha took to the hills. Maiti Nepal established prevention camps in the mountain districts that traffickers were scouring for young flesh for the brothels. Here, girls from impoverished families are given general education and awareness to resist the guile of traffickers, and vocational skills to offset the poverty that sends so many into the sex trade.

Prevention alone does not suit Anuradha's radical style. 'We can prevent, prevent, prevent and still the traffickers are going to slip through,' Anuradha says. 'I want to catch them in the act.' So Anuradha set up transit homes along the border of Nepal and India, in the cities through which the traffickers must carry their prey. Maiti Nepal's transit homes are half-way houses where girls who've escaped from the brothels wait to be reunited with their families. At the border crossings, the girls work with the police, helping them apprehend suspicious characters travelling with innocent victims.

In the last few years, Anuradha has been reaching down into the brothels themselves. Working with Indian 'brothel-busters', Maiti Nepal has given shelter to more than 60 rescued girls, the majority of them minors, and the majority of them HIV-positive. Back at the Maiti Nepal shelter in Kathmandu, Anuradha and police officials team up with the girls to identify their traffickers.

Although traffickers may be apprehended, there are few happy endings for the girls of Maiti Nepal. Few can return to their families, and in South Asia there is no place else to go. They are guaranteed shelter at Maiti Nepal for the rest of their lives—which may be only a few more years. 'When I get older, I want to go back to my village and teach art,' says Padma, a shy 14-year-old who was trafficked to Mumbai at the age of nine. Now in the early stages of full-blown AIDS, it is doubtful she'll ever see her village again.

— JF

Anuradha Koirala (right) comforts a Nepali girl just rescued from the Mumbai brothels. The girls have been transported to the Nepal–India border and are being taken by bus to Kathmandu, where they will be reunited with their families, if possible. Eighteen of the 28 rescued girls are HIV-positive. *Central Region, Nepal.* THOMAS L. KELLY

ONE-WAY TICKET TO KARACHI

BANGLADESH and PAKISTAN

Hamida

BANGLADESH

Whenever a newcomer enters the village, Niger Sultana rushes to him, crying, 'Where have you come from? How is my beloved daughter Dukhini?' Everyone in Tappu, a Bangladeshi village bordering on India, knows that seven years ago, Dukhini was smuggled across the border in the name of marriage, and has not returned. The word *dukhini* means 'distressed one'. Niger doesn't know the meaning of her daughter's name, but the pang of the word has driven her mad. The widow Niger gave her 11-year-old daughter in marriage to Nurul Islam, who said he was an Indian citizen. She had promptly accepted the man's proposal—she was living in abject poverty and was told that she needed to give no dowry to her son-in-law.

Dukhini and Nurul Islam were married in the same way that other girls of the village had got married to Indian citizens. A simple wedding. No evidence, no documents were there; they just crossed the border the night they were married. That was the last time Niger saw her daughter.

A Bangladeshi sex worker at the door of her brothel in Karachi. Each year, thousands of Bangladeshi women are trafficked across India to Pakistan. Most end up as bonded labourers, but a large number are sent into prostitution. *Karachi, Pakistan.*
ANIS HAMDANI

Every day, many Tappu residents cross back and forth over the border to do trade in India, legal and illegal. Many who knew Dukhini searched for her, but in vain. At last, Saidur Rahman, an influential resident of the village, known for his great skill in smuggling, told Niger that her daughter had been sold to another country—Pakistan, or maybe Saudi Arabia, he did not know.

But this simple village woman would not believe it. Today, she still thinks, 'Dukhini has been married, how could she be sold? The marriage was solemnised, our village people were there, this marriage can't be a lie!'

In these bordering villages of Rajshahi Division, where Bangladesh is separated from India only by open fields or a shallow river, the women say they don't know how their husbands make their money. Seeing their nice houses, their sheds full of healthy cows, it's not difficult to conclude that they are quite well off. Some houses have a dish antenna on the rooftop. Those who are a bit influential own a motorbike.

'In spite of abundant land, people are hardly seen working in the fields,' says Shanawaj, a field educator for the Association for Community Development, a local NGO. 'Most of the men work as an informers for the border security, and some smuggle goods like saris, rice and sugar.'

Along the porous border of Bangladesh and India, 'black transport' is ubiquitous, and one can see men crossing from India in broad daylight carrying sacks of rice. Bangladeshi families pass the other way, on their way to India and Pakistan. No one is there to challenge them.

Hossain Mia, a resident of Tappu village, was in the habit of doing such things, he says. At that time, he not only smuggled goods, but also lured a few Bangladeshi girls to India on the pretext of finding them a job in a cigarette factory.

'Some of the informers work as "matchmakers",' says Hossain. 'They take girls from Bangladesh to India and force them to get married to Indian men. When they finish the job, they get a good amount of money. What happens to the girls after, well . . .' Hossain will say no more.

'Of course, women are better matchmakers than men,' Hossain adds. 'Women who come from India and Pakistan to visit to their relatives take new "hunts" back with them when they return.' Their border crossing is facilitated by gifts of saris for the security police.

In many of the bordering villages, groups of girls cross the border every day to work in cigarette and bangle factories in India. Some don't return. In five villages, 80 girls have disappeared in the last several years.

— MUNNI SAHA

THE BLACK ROUTE

East and West Pakistan are still united, as far as the transportation agents are concerned. Since the mid-1970s, Bangladeshis have been migrating to seek employment in the relatively more prosperous Islamic state of Pakistan. Today, there are around 70 colonies of 'Bengalis' in and around Karachi, numbering 1,500,000 to 2,000,000 people. Most are employed in factories, private homes, hotels and restaurants, and most live in a stateless limbo—they are illegal immigrants in Pakistan, denied social services and subject to police aggression, and they are non-residents of Bangladesh, for few left their homeland with passports in hand.

Bangladeshis have built their lives in the Karachi ghettos, raised their children and established a 'home' of sorts, but they still retain ties with their families far in the east, across '1500 miles of hostile territory'. Illegal in whichever country they stand in, they rely on an established black transportation system to move back and forth. For a fee, agents take care of their transport, food and shelter along the way, and pay their way through the layers of border guards, army and police that adhere to the shaky political boundaries of Pakistan, India and Bangladesh.

Many who ride the 'black route' are regular folk, going one way or another to visit families, do business or marry a person from a home village. Others are seeking a better life, hoping to earn more than one meal a day, and the majority of these are Bangladeshis moving west. Most migrant Bangladeshis end up abused but free in Karachi shanty towns with their relatives—but a great many become fish for the agents' nets.

Since the 1970s, the black route has been an underground link that kept distant communities in contact and provided low-wage labour for the garment factories and the fish and poultry processing plants of Karachi. Today, it is also a one-way conduit for bonded labourers, particularly women and children. In a

Women walk across the border from Bangladesh to India. The two countries share a long, open border where security forces often turn a blind eye to the operations of traffickers. *Rajshahi Division, Bangladesh.* MAHMUD

common South Asian scenario, money is borrowed for transportation, pay-offs, setting up in the new venue, and provision of a job. Or the new employer lends money to set up a house, clothe the children and stock the pantry. In either case, the job pays less than living expenses and repayment of the usurious loan, and more money is borrowed. Debt servitude. As Najma Sadeque of the Pakistan women's NGO Shirkat Gah says, 'This has ballooned into one gigantic bonded labour enterprise.'

The lowest and most painful tier of bonded labour is sexual bondage. Proportionately few—but numbering in the thousands every year—women, girls and sometimes boys travel the 'black route' to a stranger's bed. Many go to be sold, even auctioned off, as wives to poor farmers who cannot afford the bride-price of a Pakistani wife. Others are sold as second, third or fourth 'keeps' to wealthy men, often resold again and again as their owners tire of them. And still others are sold to the brothels.

— JF

PAKISTAN

'Do not go to her, she is black, hungry and Bengali,' were the words pouring into the ears of the farmer Mohammed Katiar. He had come to hire the Bengali woman Hamida from Bihar Colony, a shanty town of Bengalis and Biharis on the edge of Karachi, to labour at his farm in Thatta District.

Though only 24, this was the fifth time Hamida was to be sold by Sultan, her pimp. 'Below her belly is not a human organ, but a little lamp that you can light with your match,' were the words Sultan always uttered to Hamida's customers. Ten years ago, Sultan, her not-too-distant cousin, brought three sisters, including Hamida, from Jhunjhunpur in Bangladesh. Hamida was then 14 years old.

After reaching Karachi, she was kept in a prostitution den near the Federal 'B' area. When the den was smashed by the police in 1991, she was forcibly married to a Police Inspector who already had three wives—all of them trafficked Bengalis. One of the Inspector's wives was also a pimp, providing girls to her husband's superior officers and other VIPs. The Inspector had a special love for Hamida, which infuriated this wife. When her husband was transferred to a remote area of Sindh, she sold Hamida to a contractor for 20,000 rupees (US$ 500). When her husband returned, she told him that Hamida had eloped with her paramour in his absence. Her husband found Hamida and brought her home. His tribesmen shot the contractor dead in broad daylight on the streets of Karachi.

To repay Hamida, the Inspector brought in a half a dozen cops to rape her. They threatened to put a red-hot coin in her vagina, so she would never again be 'driven by lust' to elope with another. She was found by Social Welfare volunteers, unconscious and abandoned in the bushes near Sorajani Town. She was briefly in the hospital before the police took her into custody—on a charge of illegal immigration and adultery, which under the Islamic Hudood Ordinance prescribes for women, 'death by

Many residents of the villages along the Bangladesh-India border make a living trafficking rice, saris and other merchandise, as well as people. Women traffickers wait for a clearance signal before boarding boats to cross the river into India. *Benaople Bazaar, Bangladesh.* MAHMUD

stoning, or up to 10 years of imprisonment and whipping up to 30 strikes and/or a fine.'

To her surprise and dismay, she was visited in prison by Sultan, who offered his 'helping hand'. At first thought, she preferred jail or even death, but finally agreed to go with Sultan, who told her that he could release her for 30,000 rupees. Her two sisters were living in luxury in the Emirates, he said. When she had repaid him by selling her body, he would send her there also.

Hamida said she was like a caught fish, whose trembling was of no use after falling into the net. 'Sultan was not bad like other men,' she said. 'For him, I was like a money-printing machine, so he would take care of me.'

She earned twelve times the black bail money he'd given the police, but he never talked about the Emirates again. And she never saw her sisters again.

So she worked for Sultan. She became fond of alcohol. Sitting with her customers as they smoked hashish and drank, she would pour pegs for them, a peg for herself, and two for Sultan. Forty per cent of the money she earned went to the police.

Though she loved children, Hamida said she could never conceive a baby, although she never used contraceptives. She'd heard of AIDS, but like others, believed it to be a 'disease of the white people'. She remembers some female AIDS workers coming to distribute condoms in her brothel. She offered a condom to one of her Pathan customers, who blew it up and popped it with his fist. Everyone broke into laughter.

But one cannot laugh forever. Sultan decided, once again, to sell Hamida. He sold her to an elderly mullah for 40,000 rupees. The mullah was a kind-hearted man, but he was bisexual, Hamida remembers with a laugh. He had lost his job more than once on charges of sodomy.

Rozina (right), a child prostitute and scavenger, on a train bound for Nababgong. She came to Rajshahi with her mother six years ago. Her mother married again and abandoned her. Rajshahi Rail Station, Rajshahi Division, Bangladesh. MAHMUD

One day, he left home for Peshawar, saying he would return after six weeks. He never returned. Later, Hamida heard through some of his friends that the mullah had joined a *jihad* group in warring Afghanistan.

Married to an absent mullah and unable to do prostitution, she was living in a rented room and could not pay the bills. Once again, she was approached by Sultan. He promised he would not press her into prostitution, but would find her a 'respectable job'.

A few weeks later he brought the farmer Mohammed Katiar, introducing him as a landlord in Thatta District. She would work on his betel leaf plantation with other Bengali men and women. When she arrived at the farm, there was nobody else there. Mohammed told her directly that she'd been sold to be his wife.

She swears she can never forget her first boy friend, and her first sexual experience with him when she was in Class Nine in Saidpur, Bangladesh. Sometimes her mind would get lost, and she'd see her first love in the faces of her customers. She curses, hates and loves them. Now she wishes she had always suffered from AIDS, so that even the next generation of her clients would have contracted the lethal disease. 'Less than a single drop of my blood would have been enough for them.'

— HASAN MUJTABA

BY MUNNI SAHA & HASAN MUJTABA
PHOTOGRAPHS BY MAHMUD & ANIS HAMDANI

AWARENESS IN THE TRAFFICKING BORDERLANDS
Association for Community Development

When Salima Sarwar founded the Association for Community Development (ACD) in 1990, she thought she'd be dealing with farmers and trees. The small Bangladesh NGO, which works in Rajshahi Division, lying along the Indian border, was created to help small farmers earn a living from village and farm forestry. While talking with the farming families, ACD Field Educators became aware that a silent emigration of girls was taking place. In some of the families, all young girls were simply missing. When one of the Field Educators questioned a family about their absent daughter, they showed him a letter she had written to her family from Delhi. Seeing the address, the Field Educator knew where she was—in a brothel.

So ACD found itself with another component to their tree plantation programme: trafficking prevention. Working with minimal funding, minimal training and only the confidence of the villagers as their asset, ACD has entered the bordering villages on a new footing. Most of the inhabitants of these villages are abjectly poor, and depend on 'black transportation' of rice, saris and other goods across the border to feed their families. Many of the 'transporters' have become ACD members, taking small loans for commercial enterprise. Their connections with the police and border security forces and their trust in the organisation helps ACD track some of the village girls—for a while.

'Zarina was working in a cigarette factory in India,' they might say, 'but now she's gone somewhere else.' All bits of information ACD keeps on record—although these records have little value without support from the police and government on both sides of the border.

ACD now conducts awareness programmes for villagers on the dangers of trafficking and the methods of traffickers, particularly the ruse of fake marriages. 'What is trafficking? What could happen to a girl who goes to India?' they ask the parents, the girls and the transporters. Eighty-five per cent of the villagers are illiterate—to them marriage is a vow, a social institution, not a contract. ACD educates villagers on marriage registration—how to acquire papers on the 'husband' that may someday be used to retrieve the stolen daughter.

'No one could imagine how easy it has become to get trafficked,' says Salima Sarwar. 'This is why we created the awareness programme, and why we have made the "middle persons" our members. Through them, we make the villagers aware. The rate of marriage without registration and with Indian citizens has been remarkably reduced.'

Reduced, perhaps, but only in a few tiny villages on an open border hundreds of miles long.

— MUNNI SAHA

Village women and children gather to watch a open-air drama on the dangers of trafficking, organised by the Bangladesh NGO Association for Community Development. *Tappu, Lacchmanpur, Bangladesh.* MAHMUD

4

Born Under A Bad Sign

Communities on the Edge

Just as South Asia is distinguished by its 'caste system', it is also distinguished by having numerous discrete communities that conduct sex work. Some of these communities are 'small castes', somewhere at the bottom of the orthodox caste hierarchy, and others are ethnic or tribal groups. Very few, if any, are known historically to have been solely dedicated to prostitution.

In the caste system, the segregation of communities is enforced by powerful social, religious and occupational traditions. Higher castes occupy or have access to the more lucrative and influential professions, which are often closed to the lower castes. For those at the bottom of the caste hierarchy, there may be nowhere to go but further down.

Generally, communities resort to sex work out of economic necessity when their traditional occupations can no longer support them. Some groups, such as the Badi of Nepal, have a long tradition as entertainers. For the Badi, sex work was occasionally a peripheral source of income. When television and film ended the demand for their dancing and singing, and caste exclusion kept them from receiving education or taking up other forms of employment, many—though not all—entered sex work.

The region's tribal communities have been marginalised for centuries, and in the past many have responded by eking out a living making crafts, selling low-grade plant or animal products, or conducting street performances. As these tenuous sources of income dry up in 'modern' South Asia, some of these communities have turned to sex work. Similarly with the *hijra* transgendered communities—there is little demand for their ritual or performance skills, and the traditional territories in which *hijra* 'families' collected alms have been erased by urbanisation.

Once a community, like an individual, has entered sex work, there are few opportunities for rising to even an approximation of its former dignity. It is labeled firmly and irrevocably by the public voice—with strong reinforcement by the media—as a 'fallen caste', and social and economic ostracism keeps it in place.

Communities may join the greater society in branding themselves as sex workers. Having entered sex work, they often attempt to normalise the profession within their community. Tribal groups in particular have created pseudo-histories, myths and rituals to justify in religious and historical terms how and why they have 'fallen'.

Hijras entertain at a wedding celebration. *Qissa Khawani, or the Storytellers Bazaar, Peshawar, Pakistan.* THOMAS L. KELLY

When a community adapts to a 'caste occupation' of prostitution, the social and economic relationships of its members change. As the women take over the role of wage-earners, the men become dependent, often show less inclination to work, and actively support the practice. Similarly, the responsibility of caring for aging parents is taken on by the women, and parents reinforce their daughters' engagement in sex work. In some cases, as in the Bedia tribals, women who conduct sex work are not allowed to marry, so as not to lose the income from their labour.

For a female, birth into a sex worker community is usually a one-way ticket to the bedroom. Few of the children, male or female, have an opportunity for education—and those who have, suffer ostracism in school and have few opportunities for employment if they complete their education. Children are raised in a milieu of sex work and accept the inevitability of becoming prostitutes or pimps. Girls are often initiated into the trade at a very young age to start earning earlier, and so that the family can collect a larger 'virgin fee' from the first client. These days, rural children and adults are often sent to work in urban brothels—they may enter the community's own brothel or be sold to an agent.

The members of sex worker communities, however, have some opportunities for change and support that are lacking for individual sex workers. In many rural or town sex worker communities, business is conducted in the home. The roles of pimp and madam are taken over by

Tatalau, now 79, is among the last of the Badi who performed as a classical singer and dancer. 'The girls today are like the wind. They do not have the patience and discipline necessary for classical music. That is why they have to prostitute themselves.' *Midwestern Region, Nepal.* THOMAS L. KELLY.

family members, and the daughter is looked after—for the family's income depends on the maintenance of her health and beauty.

The collectivisation of sex workers for their health and support, now beginning in some South Asian brothel areas, is often much easier in sex worker communities as they are integral groups and are often able to articulate their needs. Interventions can sometimes be quite effective. For example, the Badi community of Nepalgunj, Nepal, before it was expelled from the city in 1997 by 'concerned citizens', showed a rapid acceptance of safe sex practices, with parents negotiating condom use with clients on their daughters' behalf. Communities can also be mobilised to take pride in their own history and culture, which can stimulate them to take steps to improve their situation. Unfortunately, with externally-generated interventions there is a catch-22. External focus on a community that conducts prostitution labels it as such, and makes the struggle of their children to escape the branding of 'prostitute' even more difficult.

— JOHN FREDERICK

HOME ECONOMICS

Bimala

NEPAL

Originally, the Badi were a musician caste. The men played the tabla, drums and harmonium and the women sang and danced. When they were not entertaining, the men constructed drums and clay pipes, wove nets and fished the rivers, while the women begged. Originating from the middle hills of western Nepal, the Badi were categorised as members of a *saano jaat,* a 'small caste'.

During the winter months from mid-November to April, in what was called the 'season', groups would form consisting of three or four musicians, some dancers and other family members. They would travel down from the hills to the lowland Tarai, bordering on India, to provide entertainment, particularly at weddings. At the end of the 'season', the groups would return to the hills and live by begging, fishing and their village crafts. Each household had a semi-feudal relationship with a landlord and would present their goods and occasional entertainment in exchange for crops.

In the village where Bimala, an 18-year-old Badi woman lives, nobody under the age of 30 can play a musical instrument. The instruments were sold for family survival long ago. Few boys learn the traditional skill of drum manufacturing or may be seen weaving the fishing

The Badi woman Sangeeta, 18, conducts sex work to support her parents and siblings. 'The men who come to visit me are usually drunk; they just use me. I am so ashamed to do these "bad things", but we need the money.' *Midwestern Region, Nepal.*
THOMAS L. KELLY

nets for which the Badi were well known. Bimala's brothers learnt none of the skills associated with their caste, and work as labourers and security guards in India or selling sweets in Nepal.

The life experiences of the men and women of the Badi community stem from a complex historical and social interplay through which they have become increasingly marginalised. Their marginal status derives from their lowly caste position and their lack of access to land, education, health care and cultural capital. The fact that many Badi women are now sex workers has further isolated the community as a whole. Sex work, although offering some economic solutions to widespread poverty in the community, has given a moral edge to the historical discrimination faced by the Badi—with harassment and intimidation granted a moral legitimacy.

As with other families in the community, Bimala's parents migrated to the Tarai some 30 years ago. Bimala was born in a rural area where her parents owned a small amount of land that they had cleared. This land was later sold and the family led a peripatetic existence between the rural village where they now reside and towns such as Nepalgunj, a district centre in midwestern Nepal. Her early memories are happy ones and she recalls playing with friends and going on picnics.

'I was a beautiful child with curly hair. The high castes and "big" people played with me and gave me rupees when I danced. My father made drums and my mother

Some of the Badi maintain their traditional occupation as itinerant dancers and musicians, sometimes travelling as far afield as Tibet. *Purang, West Tibet.* THOMAS L. KELLY

begged. And then we came here to this village and we did *pesaa* (business, meaning sex work). Later, my father died.'

The drift of the Badi into sex work and much of their migration to the Tarai are related to the social and political changes within the Himalayan kingdom over the last 50 years. As the traditional economic power base of the large landowners and rulers of small principalities eroded, the patronage of the Badi declined. The gradual eclipse of their historical entertainment role was accelerated by the introduction of modern forms of entertainment such as radios and cassette recorders.

Today, economic survival is determined along gender lines, with men migrating for work both within Nepal and to India and many women working in prostitution—work that has at times been described by observers and local high-caste people as the 'caste occupation' or 'traditional work' of the Badi.

For the Badi, the marginality of their caste position is highlighted by the community engagement in sex work. In Nepal, as elsewhere, 'prostitute branded women' are placed in the lowest and most profane category and, over the last decade, focus on the Badi has tended to further stereotype and stigmatise the community. In many of the writings and media representations related to prostitution in Nepal, women of the community are portrayed in terms of both deviant sexuality and deviance from the Nepali ideal. Thus it is now widely assumed that all Badi girl children become prostitutes and produce 'fatherless' children, while men of the community are seen as having 'no traditional service' and as living off the earnings of their daughters and sisters.

The dangers and problems often represented as being inherent in a life of prostitution are less evident within the Badi community than in other sex worker communities of South Asia. In general, the sex work engaged in by Badi women takes place within a tightly-bound community in which women live in their family homes and encounter few of the standardised characters, such as madams, pimps and *goondas* (hoodlums) who figure in tabloid narratives on prostitution in India and Nepal.

The Badi of Bimala's village, around 200 people, reside on one street on the outskirts of town, a street known locally as 'Moonlight Chowk.' Bimala lives in one of the few *pakkaa* cement houses on the street. Families with daughters who are sex workers are able to have a relatively more affluent life than those without. As one community member noted when talking about a man with a large house, 'He is very rich—he has many daughters.'

Bimala is the youngest in a large family and the joint household is a full and noisy one, with several babies and young boys and girls—the children of the household daughters and daughters-in-law. For the women of this household, life is little different from that of other local women—cooking, feeding and cleaning for a large family. At first light, the women are washing at the outside pump and lighting cooking fires. Later in the day, Bimala's sisters and sisters-in-law may get a chance to sit around with other community women and gossip or play cards for small amounts of money while the children play around them. In contrast to the daughters-in-law of the household, Bimala and her sisters who do sex work are well dressed and wear make-up, waiting for any clients who may turn up.

Married women do not, as a general rule, engage in sex work and women who are working may be described as *bigriyo* (ruined or spoilt). While sex work is a social norm in the Badi communities that engage in that activity, it is not a moral norm. The moral ideals of the community are in line with the Nepali social order, with representations of ideal female behaviour reflecting this wider world.

Parents would not arrange a son's marriage with a *bigriyo* girl. Young women who marry into the family are placed low in the family hierarchy and adhere to social norms such as maintaining spatial distance from their husband's elder brothers. The position of the women working in sex work is anomalous as they are *bigriyo* on an ideal level, yet it is their income that provides primary family support. There is no moral censure attached to the practice of sex work, rather a pragmatic acceptance of its necessity for economic survival.

'My mother and father wanted me to marry but they were too poor. If there was land, who would do this work? Some people think it's bad, but women do it by necessity—it's eating and clothing work. I've been doing *pesaa* for two years and it's better with money.'

Bimala's life is circumscribed by her caste position, her lack of education and the moral world in which she lives. With all Badi women viewed as sex workers, it is difficult to step outside the localised framework of discrimination based on caste and ideology. When some Badi women were given training as sewing instructors, other caste groups refused to attend classes with them.

'When I was younger I didn't know that I was "small caste". I was innocent. Before, I didn't understand, but now it's fallen on my head. I found out when a group of us were going to the temple and a big-caste person stopped us from going inside. He said "Wait, we have to go in first," and we said, "We are all humans and if we cut our fingers, you'll bleed and we'll bleed." '

With the income from their daughters' work, Bimala's family bought a house in the urban centre of Nepalgunj, where until a few years ago there was a large Badi population in an area called Gagangunj. This asset, however, is now denied to the daughters of the house due to the moral campaigns waged by 'concerned citizens'.

After a decade of disputes over the presence of sex work in a local social space, in 1996 a moral pogrom erupted in which Badi women and children were abused and assaulted, husbands and brothers were beaten, clients were harassed and local youths mounted a patrol to prevent access to the community at night. A Neighbourhood Improvement Committee was formed with the aim of driving sex workers from the area.

Today, a small Badi population remains in Gagangunj, while the majority of sex workers have moved on to other sites with their dependent families. On a recent trip to Nepalgunj when her mother needed medical treatment, Bimala was able to stay in their house for only two days before being pressured to leave the area.

For Bimala, there are few choices in life. She is young and very attractive and may end up marrying either a boyfriend/client or having a 'love marriage' with someone in the Badi community. One of Bimala's fantasies is to own a beauty parlour, but realistically this is unlikely to happen. Apart from the economic difficulties in starting a business, few women from the wider society would choose to go to the beauty parlour of a Badi woman who has been a sex worker.

'It was my own choice to do *pesaa*. Life was hard. Two sisters were doing *pesaa* and others were eating and wearing clothes. I saw my father was poor and I decided to work and my life was destroyed. But not by my parents. I was the one who damaged my own life.'

BY LINNET PIKE
PHOTOGRAPHS BY THOMAS L. KELLY

In the Badi households that conduct sex work, parents usually take good care of their daughters. Most of the young girls in these households expect to continue in their mothers' profession. *Midwestern Region, Nepal.* THOMAS L. KELLY

ALTERNATIVES TO A LIFE OF SEX WORK
Social Awareness for Education

It is 6:30 a.m. in Gorahi, a village tucked away in a quiet valley in Nepal's western hills. Dressed in a faded petticoat, her hair woven into a loose braid, eight-year-old Poonam is busy washing dishes. Her friends pick beans in the front garden or quietly chatter upstairs in their dormitory. Poonam joined this hostel just three months ago and is the newest of the 30 girls.

The simple brick house where Poonam lives is one of seven hostels operated by Social Awareness for Education (SAFE), an NGO dedicated to supporting the Badi and other 'small-caste' communities. In 1995, SAFE opened an office in Gorahi for the underprivileged castes of the Dang Valley. Soon after SAFE arrived in Dang, Badi sex workers expressed their hopes that their children would be spared the ostracism of their caste and profession, and a year later the hostel was opened.

At 10:30, the girls walk down the road to the government primary school. New in school, Poonam is still shy and depends on the support of her more experienced 'sisters'. In her village, none of the Badi girls was allowed to attend school. She is the first girl of her community to receive an education.

Several things have contributed to the success of the SAFE hostels. Not only have they been initiated at the mothers' request, but the women are required to actively support their children. The mothers provide clothes and all the children's food, which is usually brought to the hostel after being cooked at home.

'As well,' says Dilip Pariyar, President and co-founder of SAFE, 'The hostel is a creative learning environment, and mothers can see this right away. The children can freely talk with their parents about their fears, about violence at home and other things.'

Although now insulated from sex work, some of the children in the hostels are reaching the age of 17. They must soon go back into the world. While they have been given vocational training, employment prospects for women are poor—and sex work pays more than almost any other job. Dilip is sanguine about the realities that the children will face.

'Even if later in her life, the girl enters the sex trade, she will have received an education, she will be able to make informed choices, she may be less exploited ... and she will be an adult.'

In the afternoon, Nirmala the hostel matron sits talking with some of the girls on their beds in the upstairs dormitory. They talk about their school day, their families, and their hopes for the future. Nirmala asks the girls what they want to do 10 years from now. Most of them immediately reply that they want to be teachers. One shyly admits that she wants to be a nurse. This is the first generation of Badi girls to go to school—and these dreams alone are a sign of tremendous change.

— CLIFF MEYERS

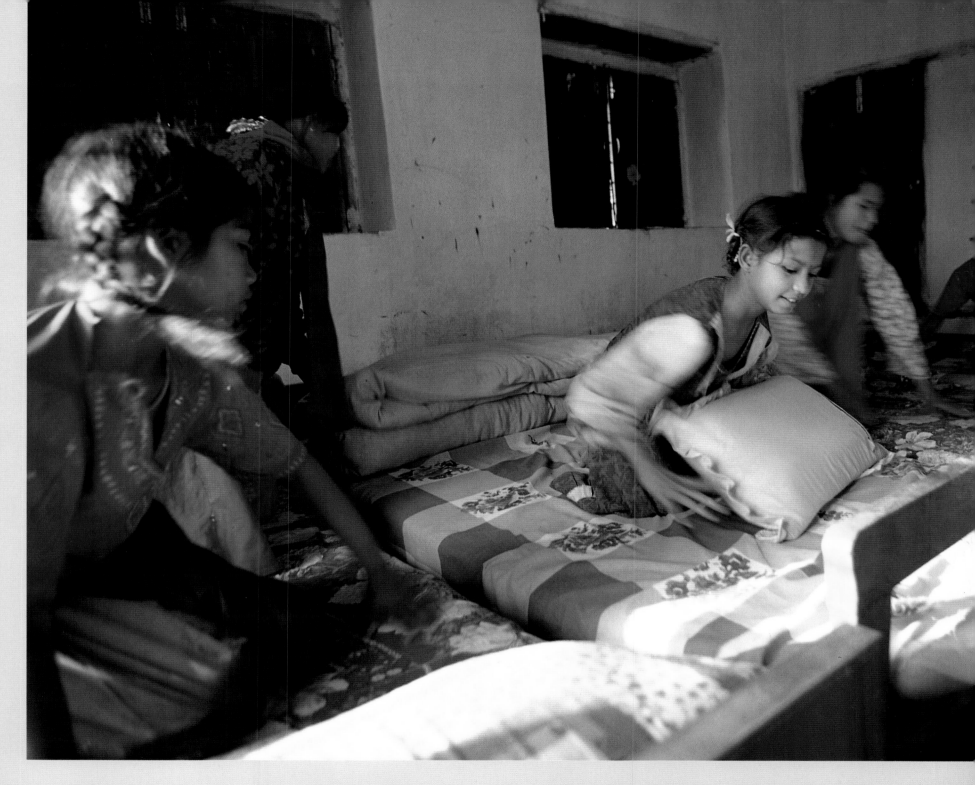

Children of the Badi community in the dormitory of their hostel, operated by the NGO Social Awareness for Education. *Midwestern Region, Nepal.* THOMAS L. KELLY

DRUMMED OUT OF THE TRIBE

Geeta + Rajendra

INDIA

We had barely settled in our chairs in Geeta's modest home in the small district town of Shivpuri, when she held out some laminated papers to us. It was clear that these were her most valued possessions. We looked at the papers, and found that these were copies of her elder son's mark-sheet for his Class 12 end-of-school examination. She proudly pointed out to us an aggregate percentage of 83 per cent.

Geeta, ravaged by her long years of sex work, looks much older than her 33 years. Her husband Rajendra is not much bigger than her elder son. Together they have fought a courageous battle against beliefs and practices of their own community that they regard as intolerably inhuman and unjust. Though they are now exiled from their community—a community itself ostracised by the mainstream world—they cannot shed their identity with it. Thus they find themselves extremely alone, and often at the edge of despair. At such times, it is the precious laminated mark-sheet, and their sons' caring support, that restore them.

Geeta and Rajendra belong to the Bedia tribal caste, which even today widely practises a little-known form of ritually-sanctioned sex work. In the shadow of feudal rural society in the state of Madhya Pradesh, young Bedia girls enter prostitution only because of the accident of

A thirteen-year-old Bedia prostitute in the red-light area of her town. In the background, Bedia men relax with the local constabulary. Madhya Pradesh, India. ANITA KHEMKA

their birth into the caste. Women are the principal income-earners of the family, whereas the men do little more than solicit clients for their daughters, sisters or mothers, engage in petty crime or remain idle.

The Banjara and Bedia are the principal castes of Madhya Pradesh in which ritually-sanctioned sex work is widely prevalent. There is evidence to suggest that prostitution is of relatively recent origin among these communities. Prior to the British Raj, nomadic tribes, including the Banjara and Bedia, were used by India's warring princely states for reconnaissance, espionage and the entertainment of troops. They also engaged to some extent in sex work, although this did not have ritual and social sanction, and was practised in a covert fashion.

With the advent of British colonial power in India, the power of the princely states broke down, and the military utility of the nomadic tribes became obsolete. In these changed circumstances, they took to organised looting and banditry as their principal means of livelihood. They came to be greatly feared, and their marauding seriously hampered the caravan trade of Western India.

The British administration classified the Bedias and Banjaras as the 'criminal tribes'—the *jarayampesha*. In the British campaign against the criminal tribes, the police would round them up with or without justification whenever any crime occurred. This not only reinforced their nomadic character, but also resulted in the males spending large periods of time either in jail or as fugitives from the law, away from their families.

The burden of supporting their families fell directly on the women. Since they lacked any skills except traditional village entertainment, they were forced to sell their bodies. Initially, the men resisted the entry of their women into the profession. In time, however, the community adopted new rituals and 'traditions' to legitimate sex work as their means of livelihood. All Bedia girls were debarred from marriage and it was mandatory that they enter the profession of sex work. The community grew mainly on the strength of illegitimate children.

Today, some Bedia daughters marry young men of their community, and the women themselves are relatively free to choose whether to enter sex work or marriage. Since they are the principal breadwinners, they enjoy a high degree of independence and control within their families and community that is not found in other caste groups. The social status of women practising sex work is often higher than that of married women, and the initiation of a daughter into sex work is an occasion for family celebration on the scale of a wedding.

In the past, Bedia women were frequently taken as mistresses by the rural rich, remaining monogamous and loyal to their main economic supporter. Today, they span the economic spectrum, ranging from those engaged in urban sex work, with high incomes and visible consumerist life styles, to poor highway prostitutes.

The prostitution of the Bedia community is largely rural, although many have now gone to work in the red-light areas of the cities or small district towns, such as Shivpuri where Geeta and Rajendra live. Recently, some groups of Bedia women have travelled abroad as part of so-called cultural troupes, especially to the Gulf countries, and have returned with very substantial incomes. On the other extreme, there are numerous rural settlements of Bedias who live in sparse hutments, with

hardly enough income for the bare sustenance of their families.

Rajendra was born 25 years ago into this society, to a Bedia mother in the city of Gwalior. When he was a child, she plied her trade mostly outside her house, and he did not understand how she brought home money to feed his three elder sisters, a younger brother and himself. When he was a little older, they shifted to a small red-light settlement of Bedias in the district town of Shivpuri.

His classmates shunned his company, and often openly taunted him. His teachers made no effort to disguise their disapproval and revulsion. Rajendra recalls with reverence only one teacher, Gopal Garg, who encouraged the Bedia children, and never made them feel that they were lesser people. When Rajendra entered secondary school, his mother took care not to cancel the column requiring his father's name; she entered a fictitious name, and added 'Late' before it.

However, in a small town like Shivpuri, it was impossible for Rajendra to hide his identity. There were many times when he felt humiliated, and in anguish, would fight with his mother. On these occasions, she would sit him on her lap and plead softly with him.

'What other way was there for me to bring you up? I know who your father is—a rich jeweller in Gwalior. But he will never acknowledge you. I was brought up like every Bedia woman, knowing that I must earn a living for my brothers and sons. If we don't take up this work, who will take care of the men in our families? I know it causes you shame, but I know no other way to take care of you.'

Rajendra realised how vastly at variance the ethical system of his community was with that of the rest of the world. Although the choice of a Bedia girl to enter sex work or to marry is nominally free, in practice it is deeply influenced by her socialisation and her conviction that it is primarily, almost exclusively, her responsibility to support her family through sex work. If a Bedia girl marries, there are strong taboos against her engaging in prostitution. However, such a choice is perceived to be

As his sisters, one by one, entered sex work, and many strange men came to spend nights in their home with his mother and sisters, he fully understood for the first time what it meant to be born a Bedia. The trauma was greatest when his mother admitted him to the local government primary school. She crossed out the column in his school entry form requiring his father's name, and instead entered her own. Thus he learned that he had no acknowledged father, and the gesture had announced his mother's profession to the world.

selfish, and neglectful of a woman's responsibilities to her mother and the men of her family.

More than half of Bedia men are unmarried. While the normal Indian family is burdened with dowry, a Bedia man must pay an exorbitant bride price to secure a wife, in order to compensate the bride's family for the loss of an earning member. Bedia women slave in sex work most of all to collect bride price for their sons and brothers. The same dream motivated Rajendra's mother and sisters.

Despite a shortage of brides, the strongest taboo amongst the Bedia is for a man to marry a girl who has entered sex work, for this threatens to end the income of the wage-earner, attacking the heart of an economic system by which the men benefit. Therefore, when Rajendra took to spending long hours with Geeta, a sex worker years older and distantly related, there was vociferous disapproval.

Rajendra was drawn to Geeta because amidst the murky world of cheap prostitution, she aspired secretly, fervently for a better life for her two sons. She would never tire of telling them that it was only by educating themselves that they could break free from the chains of their caste. Her elder son, born when she was 13, was not much younger than Rajendra and was slightly disabled. But he was infected from the start by his mother's obsession for books, and it was only Rajendra, whom he called 'elder brother', who could draw him away for a few minutes of play.

When Rajendra was a college student of 18, he went with half a dozen Bedia friends to a meeting of the community in the neighbouring town of Morena. The meeting, the first of its kind in the history of the Bedias, was organised by some administrators who sought to facilitate change in the community, together with Ram Sanehi, an elderly Bedia reformer. Ram Sanehi had

pursued many lonely battles against the practices of his community, and had not been chastened by years of persecution and ostracism.

Rajendra was immensely excited by the voices in the meeting, which challenged the inhumanity and injustice of a system which forced young girls into sex work. During the meeting, one Bedia girl, barely in her teens, stood up and bravely declared, 'It is not caste but one's actions and one's character that determine one's future, and I am going to prove this to the world!' In the voices of the young of his community, for the first time, Rajendra heard the breaking of chains.

Along with some friends, Rajendra organised the first-ever gathering of Bedia families for shared group introspection at Shivpuri. At the meeting, he stood up and declared openly, 'I am the illegitimate child of a Seth who will never acknowledge me. My mother and now my sisters have brought me up through sex work. This must end. And we must end it together!'

After this meeting, Rajendra at first resolved that he would never marry; he would break the vicious cycle of abject dependence of Bedia men on their mothers and sisters. But his growing closeness to Geeta and her boys, and encouragement by some sympathetic local administrators, spurred him into an unspeakable decision that would be a much more powerful indictment of the Bedia system. He declared that he would marry Geeta.

Both their families were devastated. The taboo against a Bedia man marrying a Bedia sex worker was so

powerful that it would ensure that the couple would be expelled forever from the community. To make matters worse, Geeta was much older than Rajendra, and her sons were almost his age.

However, the worst blow fell when Geeta revealed that she'd had herself sterilised after the birth of her two sons. She had resolved at that time that she wanted no daughters, for they would be drawn inexorably into sex work. This cycle of shame and pain must end with her.

That meant that Rajendra would never have children of his own. It was bad enough that he would be expelled from his community, his mother and sisters pleaded, but he could not allow the family line to end with him. Rajendra said that he would regard Geeta's sons as his own. But they argued that Geeta's sons were almost his age, and they would never regard him as a father.

Rejected entirely by their community and families, after their marriage they moved into a tiny tenement to start their new life together. Rajendra took a loan to run an auto-rickshaw, and even today, they survive from day to day on its earnings, which are uncertain and insufficient in a small town that has far more rickshaws than it can support. Local government officials promised to assist the family that had defied society, but nothing came their way. Geeta adjusted quickly to the role of a housekeeper, and encouraged her sons' studies with redoubled fervour. One saving grace was that she did not have to write a fictitious father's name on the school admission form. Her children now had a legal father.

After five years of marriage, their exile from their community remains unchanged. The mainstream of the caste is unrelenting, and the community regards the couple as dangerous troublemakers who might mislead women who are dutifully supporting their families with sex work. Their own families, however, have slowly accepted them. Geeta's mother has even given them her home to live in.

However, the small town refuses to forget their past. Today, it is impossible for the two to walk the streets without being followed by jeers and taunts. Old customers still bang on their door at night, and some months ago, a drunken group even broke down the door. They still do not have the money to repair it.

Money is always short, and it has been years since the couple recalls buying new clothes for themselves. Outside, in the same neighbourhood, Bedia families prosper on the earnings of their women. Geeta and Rajendra's family stands apart for what is regarded as their stubborn foolhardiness.

But there are no regrets within their household. Rajendra remains 'elder brother' to the boys in the privacy of their home, although they call him 'Papa' for public consumption. The boys greatly respect their parents for their courage and sacrifice, and they study hard, almost obsessively. 'It is this, and this alone, that will get you respect,' their mother intones. 'Study, study and earn the respect that no one can challenge.'

In the bleak desolation of their exile, the couple cherishes rare instances of acceptance. They recall the doctor who notified the local chemist that Geeta was like a daughter to him, therefore any of the family's expenses on medicine should be billed to him. Or the senior lawyer of the town who came to their home with an invitation to his daughter's wedding. 'Imagine,' they told me with great pride, 'the wedding card itself was worth 25 rupees.' And the lawyer said to the couple, 'There can be no greater privilege for me than that a courageous couple like you comes to the wedding to bless my daughter.'

But in the end it is the laminated mark-sheet of their elder son, showing his proud achievement of 83 per cent, and the loving ways of the children that make it all seem worthwhile. The last eight months, they have struggled and saved so that the elder boy could attend a coaching institute in Gwalior, to prepare him for the entrance examination for medical college. They dream endlessly of the day that he will hold his head high in the world as a doctor. That day, their lives will be fulfilled.

BY HARSH MANDER
PHOTOGRAPHS BY ANITA KHEMKA

After her abusive father left home, Dipika's mother married again, into a worse relationship. Dipika works as a beautician and prostitute to support her family. *Dum Dum, West Bengal.* ACHINTO

DIFFICULT CHANGES FOR THE NOMADS
Mukti Dhara Sansthan

The Banjara nomads of Rajasthan have plunged from a dignified past. Once they were large, colourful communities, living in tents and simple shelters, with animals in the thousands. For centuries, they provided the transportation for traders across India's rugged western deserts, and descriptions of their riches abound in the tales they still tell round their campfires.

Used and discarded by the India's princely states, persecuted by the British, they now live on the fringes of poor villages, providing cheap bazaar entertainment, making small crafts and stealing an occasional chicken. Today, many Banjaras are conducting sex work along the highways of Madhya Pradesh and Rajasthan.

Attorney Ratan Katyayani formed the Mukti Dhara Sansthan in 1993 after a chance visit to a Banjara community. 'I found that they had no access to education, health or shelter, no rights over land for grazing their animals. As they had no permanent addresses, they had no ration cards, no identity as citizens. After more than 40 years of independence, here were entire communities who were not considered to be Indians!'

Providing the nomads with voting rights, ration cards and legal defense, Ratan believes, will ensure the success of Mukti Dhara's primary goal, to integrate them into rural Indian society by providing them with settlements and agricultural lands. Today, more than 20,000 tribal people have been settled on unused government lands through the efforts of Mukti Dhara.

Settlement, however, has posed immense new problems. Land may be found for settlement, but employment and basic amenities such as water, health care and shelter are severely lacking—and beyond the capacity of Mukti Dhara to provide. The government has gone so far as to provide the nomads with wasteland, but has gone no further. 'It was a forest when we came here,' says Vimala, a resettled Banjara woman. 'But the state has done nothing for us. We live worse than the wild animals. The state provides them with better living conditions.'

The men are moving out in search of employment, and women like Vimala are returning to prostitution, aggravating a problem that Mukti Dhara has been trying to address. Vimala refuses to leave the land she has helped to clear, even if it means selling sex to survive.

'Prostitution by the nomads is a direct result of victimised communities, not individuals,' says Ratan. 'If steps are taken to bring the nomads into the mainstream and provide them with better alternatives, the problem of prostitution will decrease.' However, bringing nomadic tribes like the Banjara 'into the mainstream' will take more resources than Mukti Dhara or the nomads can muster. Only the government can help—by recognising the nomads as Indian citizens and responding with aid.

'Maybe it was better to live as we did,' says Vimala. 'We could camp out near the streams. At least we had water.'

— ABHA DAYAL

Many Banjara tribals were settled on government lands after they lost their traditional occupations. The Banjaras now have land but no facilities or employment, and continuing poverty has forced many women, like Kabita (left), to enter sex work. *Rajasthan, India.*
Anita Khemka

AN *ALI* OF CHENNAI

Neela

At 37, Neela is still in demand. She's maintained herself well, and can easily pass on the streets for a woman. She hasn't a trace of masculinity, the cross that most *alis* have to bear. It is this near-womanliness that always brings clients to her, and earns her up to 300 rupees (US$ 6.60) for every evening at the beach.

It's seven in the morning in Chennai (Madras), and the slum is stirring to life. Neela wakes up languorously after a late night on the sands. After a cup of tea, she goes round to her neighbours, as she does every morning, returning the loans she'd borrowed the previous day. After she returns home, she prepares lunch with Chithra, her 15-year-old 'daughter', a yet-to-be-castrated male—an *ali* in the making. Chithra also works as a sex worker at night, and dresses in a sari like the *alis* she lives with.

Hijras—or *alis* in South India—have long played an intimate role in Indian superstition, performance, psychology, ritual and sexuality. They are the third gender, beyond man, beyond woman, beyond gay, transvestite or transsexual. Just as South Asian sexuality, particularly male sexuality, defies the Western categories of heterosexual and homosexual, the *alis* transcend the Western definitions of the transgendered.

The *hijra* community is marginalised in a myriad ways: by their 'deviant' sexual behaviour and by their often outrageous public behaviour. A group of *alis* on the street is a mobile burlesque, full of banter, exposed body parts, and ribald, poetic commentary on the sexual habits of the 'straights' around them.

They stand apart from communal Asia by their unitarian spirit—for *hijras* can come from high-caste, low-caste, Hindu, Muslim or Christian families—and both Hindu and Muslim shrines are often found in the house of the same *hijra* 'family'. They are marginalised by superstitious awe, for like yogis and shamans, they occupy the feared outlands of society, and are thought to have the power to bless and curse. And they are marginalised by their poverty, for their traditional occupations, such as collecting alms, presiding at domestic rituals and blessing new-born children, have eroded. Most *hijras* must now resort to begging and prostitution to survive.

After lunch, Neela gets ready for her daytime job at an NGO working with HIV/AIDS prevention. A few years ago, she had been impressed when NGO workers came into the slums to talk with the *alis* about HIV infection— it was the first time anyone from the 'straight' world had reached out to them. She decided to join the NGO, and today she is a Field Officer and visits *alis* around the city, talking with them about sexual health and distributing condoms. After reporting into her office and replenishing her stock of condoms, she goes out into the slums where the *alis* live in their small 'family' groups.

Although the traditional roles of the 'eunuchs' of India have waned, they still retain a powerful sense of

Alis, or *hijras*, live together in families for mutual support. Each family is controlled by a 'mother' who looks after her 'daughters'. *Mumbai, India.* FAWZAN HUSAIN

community. *Hijra* 'families' are governed by a *guru*, or teacher, most often called 'mother'. The younger *hijras* are her *chelas,* or students, also called her 'daughters'.

Across the subcontinent, families are organised into lineages, not unlike those of conventional Indian tradition, presided over by a hierarchy of high *gurus*. In the past, many powerful eunuch families were granted houses and estates by local rulers, in exchange for their important participation in rituals and ceremonies. Today, for *alis* such as Neela, the family is still a vital social unit—an imperative for protection, work and social identity, and few greater misfortunes can fall upon an *ali* than being cast out of her family, for there is no place else to go.

Neela returns home by four for a short siesta and a quick gossip session with the neighbouring ladies, and by 5.30 she's primping and preening at the mirror, getting ready for her night at the beach. Today she chooses a deep blue, printed chiffon sari.

'My collection of saris is envied by all the other *alis,*' she claims. Her hair is adorned with fragrant white jasmine flowers, her all-time favourite.

'I don't step out of my house without flowers in my hair,' she says vainly. A dash of lipstick, eyeliner and the obligatory red *bindi* spot on her forehead (a sign of marital status sported by all Hindu brides) and she's ready for work.

Shortly before sunset, she hops into an auto-rickshaw with three other *alis,* all going to sell sex on the same strip: the long beach of Chennai, filled in the daytime with strollers, hawkers, family groups and food vendors, and frequented at night by men looking for sex, with males, females or *alis.*

Neela's work starts about 7.30 and goes on until about 10.30. Of the 300 rupees she may earn in a night, she pays 20 to each local policeman, with whom she maintains a cordial relationship. The local thugs also partake of 20 rupees apiece, if she doesn't pay them with sex. If she's lucky, she'll take home 150 or 200 rupees a night.

While many other sex workers rip off their clients on the sly, like picking their pockets while performing sex, Neela says she is grateful to the men that come to her, and cheating them would be unethical.

'But,' she says, 'I can be really bad if the going gets tough and I have to fight to survive.' Neela is effeminate, but she's not a lightweight. Amongst her *ali* colleagues, her tough, no-nonsense reputation precedes her.

Most of her clients believe they are having sex with a woman when they have sex with Neela. 'That,' she says, 'is my trade secret.' She fools them into believing that they are indulging in vaginal sex when there is no penetration at all.

'Most of my clients are drunk anyway,' she laughs. 'So it's hard for them to tell the difference.'

She always uses condoms, even though it is non-penetrative sex that she sells. She has been tested for HIV and as she is in the clear, she is wise enough not to take any more risks—she's seen many of her friends and peers succumb to the deadly infection.

Neela was born a boy, to a working-class family in northern Chennai. She was named Neelakantan, meaning Shiva. Growing up, Neela recalls, 'I was always playing with my sisters and indulging in "girlish" behaviour. I never played or hung around with my brothers or other

Alis dressing in festival attire. Each year, thousands of *alis* descend on the village temple of Koothandavar for the festival of Aravan. In the epic *Mahabharata*, Lord Krishna changed himself into a woman for a single night to marry the warrior Aravan before the latter's sacrifice to ensure victory in battle. *Koovakkam, Tamil Nadu, India.* THOMAS L. KELLY

Alis enjoy working the streets. Their begging style is a mobile burlesque of songs, clapping, exhibitionism and humorous comment on the sexual habits of passersby. *Mumbai, India*. FAWZAN HUSAIN

boys in the neighbourhood. I was happy dressing up with the girls.

'This peculiar behaviour of mine didn't go unnoticed by my family,' she laughs. 'I always wanted to grow my hair long, to wear lovely, fragrant jasmine flowers in my plaited hair.'

When Neelakantan was 19, one day he went alone to see a movie. During the interval, he noticed a young man with an overtly effeminate demeanour, sporting long hair plaited with flowers. This intrigued him enough to draw the man into a conversation. Sensing the curiosity and the sexual similarity in the young Neelakantan, the man invited him to his house in a slum near the Harbour area. There, he met a group of similar men—*alis,* some of whom were dressed in saris.

'Although I found their living conditions pathetic, I soon decided to join them and become part of their "family". I couldn't bear to live at home any more—my own family gave me such pressure to be "normal", to act like a boy. I was miserable.

'I could only find peace of mind when I was with my *ali* family. Joining them seemed to be the only way out of my terrible situation.'

Neelakantan's new family was headed by an *ali* called Devi who rechristianed him Neela, in keeping with the tradition in which all *alis* rename themselves or modify their names into feminine ones. Neela started cross-dressing in a sari like the others in the family, and going out with them to sell sex in the cruising areas and on the beach.

When he was about 21, Neela decided he wanted to leave and join another group of *alis* who lived near the beach. 'My new family was run by Vasanthi, and it was she who got me operated on.'

Although it is commonly believed that all *alis,* or *hijras,* are castrated males, the community spans a wide range of sexual forms. The *hijra* ideal is to have been born neither a man nor a woman—what is inaccurately known as a hermaphrodite—and traditionally the highest *hijra* gurus were those born with ambiguous genitalia. In general, those who are born male and do not undergo castration—and who often lead closeted lives as straight, married men—are known as *zenanas,* and are scorned by the *hijras* as impostors.

Hijras cannot procreate, and new family members must be recruited, often from among the *zenanas.* As they preside over the blessing of new-born children, *hijras* are also quickly aware of the presence of a child with ambiguous genitalia. In common superstition, being born a *hijra* is hereditary, so families will often quietly give their child away to the community, for fear it will affect the marriage potential of their 'normal' sons and daughters.

When Neela was about 25, she fell in love with Prakash, a young auto-rickshaw driver who lived near her house. Soon he moved in with her, and they lived together for five years. With Prakash in her life, Neela reduced her sex work, as she wanted to spend most of her time with him.

'Those were the most unforgettable, enjoyable years of my life,' Neela reminisces. 'My house was well equipped, much better than the other *alis.* We had a TV, even a fridge!

'I was so happy—until the day he got married to a girl in the neighborhood.'

Heart broken, Neela took to the bottle with a vengeance. Soon, riddled with debt, she was forced to sell all the material comforts she had acquired with Prakash and go back to her profession. She went from being one of the most envied *alis* in Chennai to just another sex worker.

It's been eight long years since Prakash walked out on her and into a woman's arms. Looking back, Neela is not bitter about that chapter in her life. To her, it was glorious.

'After all, not many *alis* get to have a "husband" like Prakash. I'm practical enough to understand that a man needs to marry and settle down to raise a family. It's something we *alis* can never give.

'Yes, I felt betrayed. I felt very angry and depressed. That's human nature. But I got over it quickly enough, I pulled myself together. Now my future is my daughter and her well-being. I know she will take care of me.'

Older and wiser, though still in the reckoning, Neela realises that it's time to move on. She doesn't have too many good years on the beach left. And working in the fight against AIDS, she says, is her calling.

'I want to do something useful in life. I'm seeing too many of my people get infected and die. I'm not just a sex worker—now I'm also a social worker. I want to help our people in any way I can.'

BY SUNIL MENON
PHOTOGRAPHS BY THOMAS L. KELLY
AND FAWZAN HUSAIN

Above: At the Aravan festival, *alis* dance at a beauty contest sponsored by the HIV/AIDS intervention NGO, Sahodaran. *Koovakkam, Tamil Nadu, India.* THOMAS L. KELLY

Facing page: At the yearly festival for Aravan, *alis* play out the role of Krishna, transformed into a woman and in mourning after the sacrifice of her husband Aravan. *Koovakkam, Tamil Nadu, India.* THOMAS L. KELLY

5

The Plague Years

HIV/AIDS

Slowing down the spread of sexually-transmitted HIV/AIDS in South Asia comes down to two power equations. The first is a personal equation: the will-power of individual men to limit their sexual activities—to abstain or have fewer partners—and to wear a condom when they are sexually active. The second is a social equation: when men's will-power is lacking, the power of the sex workers or wives to convince men to put on condoms.

Awareness of HIV/AIDS and the availability of condoms are expanding across the region, but strategies directed at changing the practices of clients are still at an early stage of development. A fair amount is known about the frequency of condom use and men's conceptions of HIV/AIDS, but very little is yet known about the attitudes and practices which discourage condom use—for example, the 'it-can't-happen-to-me' syndrome,

'macho' anti-condom peer influence, or alcohol intoxication vis-à-vis condom use.

Although many interventions are being directed at truckdrivers, students, soldiers and middle-class clients, proportionately few have been directed at working-class, illiterate or semi-literate men—the bulk of the client population—among whom are the migrant labourers who are carrying HIV from the cities into the villages.

Motivating men is difficult, because men hate condoms. Even most AIDS-aware men will try to avoid pulling the latex out of their wallets. Fear of contracting HIV often isn't sufficient motivation—and fear is further dissipated when men are intoxicated, which they often are when they visit sex workers. A few things do wake them up a bit: having been treated for an STD or knowing someone infected with HIV, but neither are the best prevention strategies.

If men won't willingly put on condoms—and they generally won't—it comes down to condom negotiation. Successful negotiation is determined by the power balance between the sex worker and client, and this depends greatly on the sex worker's status, self-esteem, support from others, and access to awareness and negotiating skills. These, in turn, are determined by the venue in which sex work takes place.

As has been shown in Calcutta's Sonagachi red-light area, within a discrete brothel area sex workers can be

Above: Santi, picked up in a police raid as a minor from Kamathipura, Mumbai, was brought to Calcutta with HIV. *Kamathipura, Mumbai.* ACHINTO
Facing page: Laughing at a brothel joke, in which a woman quietly attaches water-filled condoms to the back of a client's shirt, and lets him walk around the brothel looking ridiculous. *Daulotdia Brothel, Bangladesh.* SHEHZAD NOORANI

collectivised to defend individual sex workers in condom negotiation. As well, the power elements of a brothel district, such as pimps, madams and local thugs, can be mobilised to support safe sex practices, if they can be convinced that their business would be benefited by discouraging AIDS.

However, the 'Calcutta experiment' is not readily duplicable. Most sex workers do not work in tight, established brothel areas such as Sonagachi. And the 'unity' of the Sonagachi red-light community is exceptional. Similar efforts have been unsuccessful in the Kamathipura red-light area of Mumbai, for example, in large part due to an intransigent mafia, little sense of brothel 'community' among madams, pimps or sex workers, and a high proportion of bottom-rung establishments for lower-class clients. Many of the latter are brothels of trafficked or under-age girls, whose clients and madams are not the sort to concern themselves with safe sex.

Outside brothel areas, both HIV/AIDS awareness and negotiation support are difficult to provide for 'floating' prostitutes, which include most male prostitutes. Without peers or madams to support them, and generally selling sex to lower-class clients, floating prostitutes have minimal negotiating power. One of the tragedies of the destruction of brothel areas in Bangladesh, Nepal and elsewhere in recent years has been that thousands of women have been thrown out on the streets, and into much higher-risk situations.

In South Asia, rural sex workers in towns and villages have about the same power constraints as urban floating sex workers: lack of peer support, a poorer clientele, little access to awareness and condoms, and poverty pressing them to give in to client demands. Rural sex workers at truckstops fare little better, although more interventions are directed towards them and their clients.

Caste or tribal communities that are dedicated to sex work have some advantages. Like brothel districts, they are accessible to interventionists and can potentially be mobilised as 'communities'. Where sex work is a 'family business', the families may negotiate with clients on behalf of their wage-earning women.

HIV/AIDS interventions with male prostitutes are problematic for a number of reasons. In South Asia, there is still a general denial of the high prevalence of male-to-male sex, either casual or professional. In consequence, HIV transmission through anal intercourse is often not on the agendas of interventionists and governments. Condom acceptance from the client side is difficult because of clients' guilt, denial and concealment. Male-male oriented HIV/AIDS organisations are hard to establish because few men are willing to 'come out', except in a few urban centres.

There have been some very effective HIV/AIDS intervention programmes in South Asia, but many are not duplicable outside the area where they have been developed. Of greater concern, South Asia has insufficient capacity to bring any interventions—except for radio and television—to scale, to place them in every city, town and village of a land with an immense rural population.

— John Frederick

Shalini (left) is sick with tuberculosis and possibly AIDS. She entered prostitution after her husband abandoned her with three children. Shalini lives at home with her mother (right) in Kultani, a poor fishing community that supplies many women to the Calcutta brothels. *Kultani, West Bengal.* ACHINTO

WOMAN OF WELCOME BROTHEL 52

Jyoti

INDIA

It is Sunday afternoon in Brothel 52. Light tropical sunshine slips in through the curtains, and the neighbourhood is slowly limbering up for the evening. Jyoti has just awoken, finished her bath and spent half an hour at the mirror dressing her hair and making up her face. She relaxes on one of the brothel's gaudy, overstuffed sofas, watching television.

Jyoti is fortunate. After 12 years in the trade, she is still beautiful. Unlike many women of Mumbai's Kamathipura district, her eyes are bright, she has no visible scars, no addictions. She belongs to one of the city's better brothels, has paid her debts to the brothel owner, and saves her money.

'I am from Karnataka, in South India. My father was a poor farmer, and my mother died as soon as I was born. I'm the youngest of four sisters, and I always knew my father could never afford my dowry. Still, I had a happy childhood. I used to play in the fields and go to the village fairs. I studied up to Class Three. I can write my name in Hindi and I can even read the newspaper.'

Today, Jyoti is dressed in a skirt and blouse of soft pastel colours, embroidered with flowers. Her black eyes are lined with sparkle. She wears thick silver anklets, a silver nose ring, and cheap, imitation ear studs. An amulet, for luck she says, is tied round her upper right forearm,

Mumbai sex worker Geetanjali relaxes in the afternoon before work. *Kamathipura, Mumbai.* THOMAS L. KELLY

another round her waist. The red nail polish on her toenails and fingernails is chipping away.

At 25, she is old for her profession, but still commands the same price that she did at 16. Her waist is slim and her hips are big enough, as the Indians would say, to bear a thousand sons. She has burn marks on her left breast and her inner thighs, inflicted during her 'training period'. They don't lower the value of her body, but every day when she bathes, they remind her of her inexplicable fate, and the life that was taken from her as a child.

'When I was ten years old, my father's friend, whom I trusted very much, took me out to a field. He called his friends and they gang-raped me. I was left there bleeding. From that time, my life went for a toss. My father died and my step-mother married another man. I was beaten every day. I wanted to kill myself, but I just couldn't. Then I met a man who said he would give me a job in a big city. I was so unhappy then—I wanted to die or run away. So I went with him.'

'He brought me to Mumbai and sold me to a brothel. I think he got Rs. 10,000 (US$ 220). I was 13 years old.'

In a couple of hours, her customers will troop in: businessmen, minor government officials, long-time lovers—those who can afford Jyoti. All will use condoms, or will be asked to leave.

'This is my fate. There is no way out now. But it could be worse. All the men think I'm very beautiful. Many of them want to marry me. Many have wives and children, but they say they will leave everything behind if I say yes.

They take me out for films, give me good food and take me to the doctor if I fall sick.'

In the street below, leaning against the doorways of their 'cages', are the women who serve those who cannot afford Jyoti. Many have been trafficked from Nepal—low-priced imports for students, truckdrivers, sailors, junkies and construction workers. They wear thick, white pancake makeup, with their eyebrows crudely blackened, and dress in cheap, bright dresses, often with long sleeves to hide their scars. When their clients refuse to wear a condom, they can't turn them away. The men are often drunk and could make problems, and the girls need the money.

Kamathipura is home to thousands of women from the little towns of India and Nepal. Called by a variety of circumstances, most end up in the legendary 'cages' or in the more affluent 'welcome' brothels like Jyoti's. Many are mere children, still trying to fathom their isolation.

The first few days are the worst. Most of the girls have been cheated by friends and family, lured by promises of big money and better living. They are broken into the trade with a ferocity generally reserved for wild animals. The stubborn, those looking for escape, are brutally savaged.

'In the beginning, I resisted when the men came to me. Then a local goonda "trained" me. He burnt me on my breasts and thighs and raped me again and again. I cried a lot. My madam gave me a lot of affection. She said she had also gone through the same experience and showed me her scars. She said it was best I stopped resisting and enjoyed my destiny.'

Within weeks they begin to dismember their past; it is the only way to survive.

'My madam was a very nice woman. She treated me well and gave me clothes, good food, perfume, oil and a lot of love. I'd never been loved in my life. I used to sit on her lap and play with her. For the first time, I had somebody to talk to.'

In time, everybody falls into line. As the months slip by into years and the girls become women, they learn to adapt. Not all are as fortunate as Jyoti. Many take to drugs and alcohol to soften the pain, and now many are waiting for death from HIV/AIDS.

The brothel district of Kamathipura began in the late 17th century. Originally, this part of Central Mumbai was inhabited by swarthy Kamathis from Andhra Pradesh who fashioned bamboo for the marketplace. To meet the carnal demand of Her Majesty's troops, British authorities decided to start a full-fledged red-light area. Kamathipura was chosen and soon Chinese, Anglo-Indian, French and other 'white' women started up flourishing bordellos. To the natives, the street came to be known Safed Galli, or 'white alley'.

Twice, in 1889 and 1926, efforts were made to 'legalise' the business of Kamathipura. Medical check-ups, licensing of brothels and other activities were initiated to check the proliferation of prostitutes. The government soon found this economically burdensome and in 1929 stopped their attempts at regulation.

Legalisation soon gave way to prohibition. In the 1930s, India joined the League of Nations and seriously sought the abolition of the sex trade. Police and magistrates were given new powers, and though prostitution was scarcely diminished the sex workers came under the arbitrary control of the cops on the street.

When Morarji Desai took the reins of the erstwhile Mumbai State in the 1950s, sex work in Kamathipura once again became the target of 'moral rectification'. In 1956, India passed the Suppression of Immoral Traffic in

Women and Girls Act (SITA), which aimed to regulate the flow of new girls into the sex trade. As with similar legislation throughout the world, SITA did not succeed in limiting prostitution. Instead, the Act effectively criminalised prostitution, marginalising the sex workers and making them greater victims of pimps, hoodlums and the police.

Somehow, through the years Kamathipura has parried the legal strictures placed on other Indian red-light areas and has steadily grown in size and importance. In part due to the regulatory activities which criminalised sex work, a powerful sub-culture has emerged—a hierarchy of pimps, brothel owners, organised criminals, police and politicians, sharing the big money of the sex industry. Today, the economic structure of Kamathipura is well defined and all profit from it—except the sex workers themselves.

Kamathipura is a maze of tiny, cluttered lanes. Over 20,000 prostitutes—female, male and transsexual—work on Lane 1 and from Lanes 7 to 14. On Lanes 2 through 6 are shabby residences of lower middle-class families, who eke out a living in the respectable world. Despite this mix of white and black worlds, harmony is the essence of Kamathipura. When Mumbai was rocked by the communal riots of the early 1990s, the area was quiet. Hiding within the blackness of its soot-covered walls, Kamathipura only wept. There was enough pain here; anger had no place.

'Welcome' brothels along a lane in Kamathipura. Welcome brothels are middle-class establishments, in which the women have a relatively better life than those who work in the nearby 'cages'— the cheap brothels which service working-class men.
Kamathipura, Mumbai, India. THOMAS L. KELLY

On the average, each brothel has eight to 10 girls. About 20 per cent of them are below the age of 18, and 20 per cent are above 40 years old.

'In this place there are 15 girls,' says Jyoti. 'We take care of each other. If a girl is sick or needs any kind of help, everybody contributes. We are all in the same boat. We have no mothers or fathers or family. We only have each other.'

According to a survey of Kamathipura sex workers, one third of the girls have been abducted from home and sold to the brothels. Fifteen per cent reach the cages thanks to the *devadasi* system, in which religion provides divine sanction for sexual exploitation. The majority of Kamathipura sex workers, however, have not been trafficked—they are victims of poverty, abuse and social ostracism: 10 per cent have been abandoned by their husbands; 8 per cent were raped as children, excluding them from arranged marriage; and 6 per cent were the victims of incest. A small, sad 8 per cent are the daughters of prostitutes.

There is a wide range of venues for sexual activity in Kamathipura. Welcome brothels such as Jyoti's have a comfortable sitting room to entertain waiting clients, curtains on the windows and clean linen on the beds. More affluent clients frequently spend a half hour or more with the sex workers.

'The only problem is that I have to sleep with any man who comes to me. Sometimes the men are ugly. They stink of alcohol, bad breath and sweat. But I'm a prostitute. It's my job. I can't say no.'

As they get older, sex workers lose most of their income as their clients go to younger women. The struggle with poverty begins at a time when many are trying to raise their children. *Kamathipura, Mumbai.* THOMAS L. KELLY

The low-priced cages are tiny squalid rooms, decorated as best the women can afford. Peripheral entertainment is not provided, and clients may spend only five or ten minutes with the sex workers—perhaps the world's shortest 'short-times'.

If the life of the women of the cages is rough, it is rougher still for those who work on the fringes of Kamathipura and the other red-light districts of Mumbai. These women hang out at bus stops, lonely lanes, railway stations and wherever men congregate. The sexual act can take place anywhere: in cheap hotel rooms, under parked lorries, on the pavements, or under the staircases of dilapidated buildings. The sexual act is furtive. No time is wasted on niceties, and condoms are not mentioned.

Jyoti's Brothel 52 is a comfortable, middle-class welcome brothel. Comparatively, hers is a privileged existence. She has regular medical check-ups and has been introduced to condom use. On the streets below, as many as 50 per cent of the women and girls are HIV-positive.

'I don't know what my future is. I know about AIDS, but I've never fallen seriously ill and I always insist on condoms. My madam supports it. If they don't put it on, they can go elsewhere. My real lover doesn't use condoms. I think—I hope—that he only sleeps with me. I don't mind getting pregnant with his child. I will love it, I want a child so much.'

The prostitute's life is a life of constant sexual interaction and rare, if ever, sexual communion. For many sex workers, abused by men in a thousand circumstances, the thirst for love is deep and obsessive. Many have cut their wrists and jumped from buildings in an attempt to end their lives after broken love affairs. Jyoti is lucky; she has a man who reciprocates her feelings, a man she has been able to trust—so far.

Trust in men is not a common trait in sex workers and for most, a child is the only family they can ever have. Few want to return home. Home is Kamathipura.

'I returned to my village once with my lover. I didn't like it. There's no money there. Everyone is poor. The farmers have to wait for the monsoon, which never comes. My life here is better. I've got few problems, and all the girls in the lane are my friends. I've been here for 12 years and I'm senior now. I've saved a lot of money and maybe one day I will leave this line, marry my lover and start a family. Where? I don't know. Somewhere where nobody knows me.'

BY RAJENDAR MENEN
PHOTOGRAPHS BY THOMAS L. KELLY

Two sex workers, Bishakha and Geetanjali, with their madam (centre). Sex workers have ambivalent relationships with their madams—while madams often keep their sex workers in debt servitude, they also give them affection as well as protection from clients and police. *Kamathipura, Mumbai.* THOMAS L. KELLY

EMPOWERED NEGOTIATIONS
The STD/HIV Intervention Programme

During the early afternoon, when most of the sex workers of Calcutta are relaxing, washing laundry and tending to their children, 100 sex workers don pale green smocks and fan out into the brothel districts of the city to deliver the message of safe sex. With the support of pimps, madams and local doctors, these 'peer educators' move from brothel to street to teashop, talking with the working women, pulling flipcharts and condoms out of their bags, and sharing jokes about asking stubborn clients to leave their rooms.

In Sonagachi, one of South Asia's oldest and most venerable red-light districts, the 5,000 resident sex workers have taken their health needs into their own hands. Borne from a survey of Calcutta's sex workers in 1992, the STD/HIV Intervention Programme (SHIP) has been one of the most successful AIDS intervention activities in South Asia. In 1998, the HIV prevalence of Sonagachi sex workers was 5.5%, about one-tenth that of the women of Mumbai's Kamathipura brothel area, and one-fourth that of the sex workers of Bangkok, a city with perhaps the highest level of AIDS awareness in the developing world.

Says Dr Smarajit Jana, the epidemiologist who initiated the programme: 'All the standard intervention strategies are based on the premise that if you provide condoms and sufficient information, then people will change their behaviour practices. Here in India, condom use is not going to make it into a sex worker's day-to-day practices because she has hardly any rights over her body.

'In condom negotiation, the client has all the power, and the police, the pimps, everyone will back him up. Until and unless that sex worker has a level of confidence and a powerbase where she can fight for herself, this isn't going to be successful. If a sex worker receives support from other sex workers when she is negotiating with a client, she will negotiate more effectively.'

The project began with a primary health clinic operating out of a small room in a local men's club. The first group of peer educators was formed from the sex worker community. As the peers made their rounds of the brothels, confidence rose among the women of Sonagachi. On the sex workers' request, as of 1999, 22 clinics, womanned by peer educators, have been set up in Calcutta and the outlying towns of West Bengal.

In 1995, the Durbar Mahila Samanwaya Committee (DMSC) was established—the first collective of sex workers in South Asia. Today, sex worker unity is felt in the brothel chambers—and HIV is on the run.

'If a dispute occurs between a client and a sex worker, now she can say, "If you do like this, I will call the DMSC." Things have changed overnight, and now no clients can exert their way as they used to. Women's empowerment is not superfluous to interventions of this sort—they have to go hand in hand.'

— JF

The STD/HIV Intervention Programme began with this clinic in the Sonagachi brothel area. Here, physicians provide general health care. In another clinic, testing and counseling for HIV is conducted, but only at the sex worker's request. *Sonagachi, Calcutta.* Thomas L. Kelly

119

IN THE LINE OF FIRE

INDIA and NEPAL

When no trucks pass by, all one can hear is the rushing of the river in the valley below. Electricity doesn't come to this stretch of the mountain highway, and the little shacks squeezed between the tarmac and the cliff-edge are lit only by candles and the fires from clay stoves. It is a hot, dry summer night, a few weeks before the monsoon. Half-dressed children play up and down the road, chattering in their games, popping in and out of the roadside kitchens to fetch a Coke or beer for a sister or mother's client. On wooden cots on the narrow verandahs, small groups of women and girls talk quietly. Most are in their early twenties, some are thirteen or fourteen.

Kabita washed her hair as the sun set, and it still glistens with water as she sits on the bed behind the stove, fussing over her youngest child. Thin and feverish, the child is three years old and looks scarcely two. He won't stop crying and Kabita tries to control her irritation. He is a boy, but his hair is long and he is dressed like a girl, to protect him from evil spirits. Even the spirits have no use for girls.

Her seven-year-old stands quietly watching, wanting to help, afraid of a scolding. 'If I didn't have these, I'd be free,' Kabita says. After a while, the little child quietens down, falls asleep. Kabita is silent for a moment, and suddenly, like the moon emerging from a cloud, she

Many of Nepal's truckstop sex workers operate their own tea-stalls, from which they sell sex to passing truck and bus drivers. *Central Region, Nepal.* MANI LAMA

smiles, loosens her hair, hikes her blouse above her black brassiere to cool her back, and plunks down loosely on the floor.

'I was riding to Mugling tonight,' she says. 'But I think I'll stay here.'

Kabita is 28, one of the older women working the truckstops on this part of the mountain road west of Kathmandu. She is respected by the women, truckers and NGO workers from Kathmandu to Narayanghat—a 'queen of the highway'—known for her honesty and her tongue, a woman not to anger.

'When I was fourteen, my parents married me off. Do you think I liked it? I was the daughter-in-law, like all the others. Early in the morning I'd get up, get the sickle and basket and go out to cut grass for the buffaloes. I'd have a little popcorn in my sash to eat, that was all. All morning, every morning. I'd come home to make lunch for my husband and in-laws, then back to the fields.'

For a moment, the mountain wall across the narrow highway is eclipsed as a large, red petrol tanker rolls slowly by. The driver, bare-chested, strong, smiles and waves into the kitchen. On the seat behind him, a young girl laughs with the driver's assistant.

'Going up to Kathmandu,' Kabita says.

Sometimes the women take a ride for a few hours in one direction or the other, stopping in a wooded place along the way, and catch another truck back home later in the evening. Sometimes, like Kabita tonight, they stay in their *dhabas*—their roadside teashops—and entertain those who drop by.

'My husband and I had a shop in Delhi for about eight months, then we came back. We were together for seven years—sort of. This is my son,' she says, smiling at the older child. When she was with her husband, she had seen other women, freer women, and she'd gotten some ideas from them. 'Then he brought home a second wife. I knew what to do. I left.'

Kabita looks out at the highway, her eyes suddenly flash distant and hard. 'A couple of years later, I married again. A Magar man. He took me up and down, didn't want to settle down. A job here, a job there. I'm lucky I had friends. This is his son,' she says, nodding at the small child in the cot.

As quickly as they hardened, her eyes soften into amiability. She reaches for a metal cup, fills it half with cheap vodka, half with Coke and offers it. 'After that, I started drinking and smoking,' she smiles. She fills another cup for herself and leans back against the wall, lighting a cigarette.

Inside the tiny shop, the plates, cups and bottles of beer are arranged on the shelves in immaculate order. The floors, the stove are smooth with fresh, dry mud. Outside in the night, the candles and cooking fires dimly light the mountain wall. Children walk in and out of the shadows. A young girl, large-eyed with wild hair, pops into Kabita's *dhaba*. She is perhaps thirteen done up with touches of lipstick and eyeshadow. She grabs a beer from Kabita's shelf and disappears into the dark.

Kabita drags on her cigarette in long puffs, consuming it in a few moments. 'My girlfriend used to work in an office in Narayanghat. She'd finished Class Ten, she had a good job, she had everything. A police sub-inspector raped her. Finished. After that, he could rape her whenever he wanted to. What was she anymore? She couldn't stay, she quit her job. Now she's in Kathmandu.

Men come to her by telephone; she makes a lot of money. But then, she's free.' Kabita glances at her child in the cot.

Many of the adult women who work along the highways of Nepal are entrepreneurs, running their own tiny roadside teashops. Most started in their teens, coming first to truckstops near their village, then shifting venues every few months. In Nepal, few have been forced into the profession by traffickers or pimps. Although a girl may quickly take up a temporary 'husband' for protection when she arrives in a new place, she operates independently, usually working under an older woman who runs her own *dhaba*. Almost all the older women have children, and many have husbands. The latter are seen at the *dhabas* in the mornings, eating rice with their wives, only to disappear later in the day so as not to disturb the clients.

Women enter the truckstops, as they enter other forms of sex work, for a variety of reasons. Many, like Kabita, are the dross of a bad marriage—those with the strength and will to strike out on their own rather than submit to a formalised slavery to husbands and parents-in-law. Others come out of abject poverty or from ostracised castes, needing to support parents and siblings. Others are victims of rape. Thus spoiled for marriage, they can only expect a future of rape without payment—and some women, like Kabita's friend, decide they may as well be paid if they're to be regularly raped.

In India, women enter the truckstops for the same reasons, but enter with far less power and potential than they do in Nepal. There, the *dhabas* are usually operated by men. Women often work out of family shacks erected near the truck halts, or in patches of woods or bushes

The women and girls who work Nepal's truckstops have among the highest risk of any sex workers in the country of contracting HIV. *Central Region, Nepal.* MANI LAMA

122

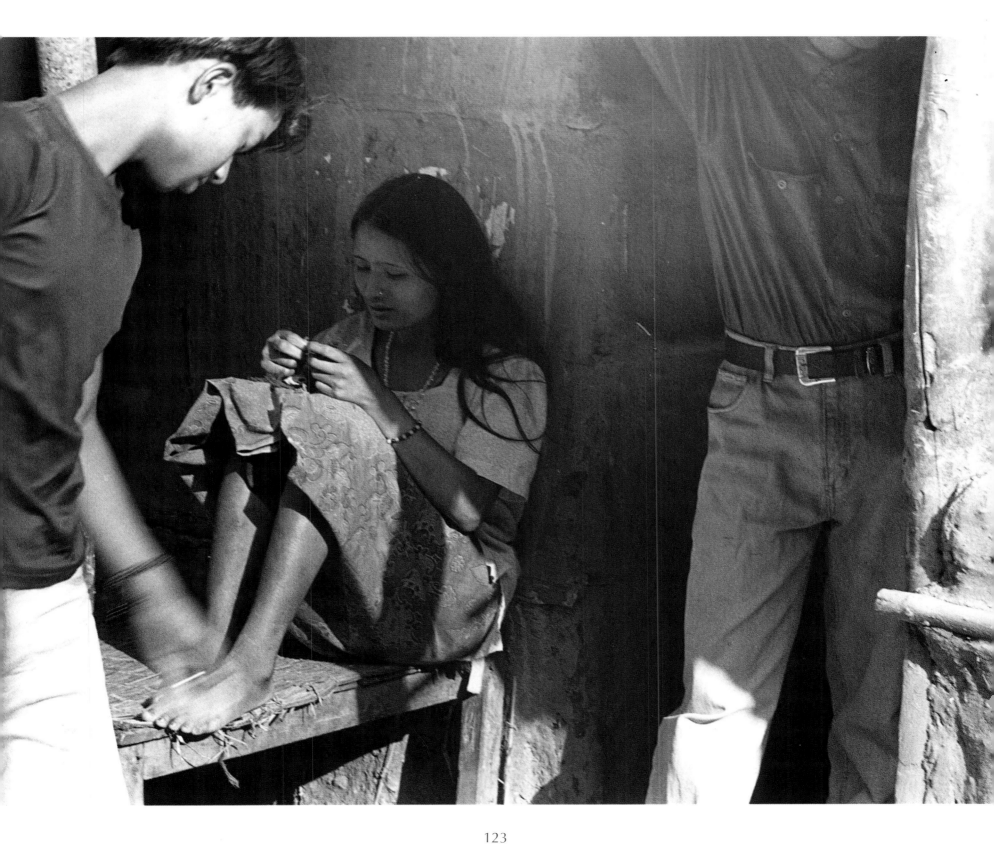

along the roads. More often victims of hoodlums, pimps and police than their Nepali sisters, Indian roadside sex workers have minimal protection from abuse, and are often paid for their services at the whim of the client.

As the evening stretches on, a few gaudily painted trucks slow and stop along the highway. It is only three hours from Kathmandu. They will spend the night here, and early the following day they will drive into the city for unloading. The drivers swing out of their trucks, followed by their assistants—*kalashis*—who quickly find the ready triangular river stones to jam beneath the tyres.

One of the drivers ducks into Kabita's *dhaba*. Her older son rushes up to him, tussles with him. 'It's hot, take off your shirt,' Kabita says. He settles down on the floor, leaning against Kabita, and they talk of the events of the three days since they've seen each other. He has to make it to Kathmandu that night he says, and asks Kabita if she would like to come along. 'No, I want to stay here tonight; Babu has a fever,' she says. He doesn't seem to mind, and asks Kabita about her little son. He's a pleasant man, doesn't drink, and talks with Kabita as if he's known her for years.

Unlike many clients of sex workers, most of the Nepali truckdrivers are respectful of the women. In a poor country, where most working men are poorly employed and poorly paid, the drivers are proud of their work and their responsibilities. For years before they got behind the wheel, all have worked as *kalashis*; they have worked hard and paid their dues. The friendly banter between males and females is there, and takes place with great animation morning and night as the men stop for meals, tea and tyre repair at the roadside halts. But the smirks of the streetboys

Bengali roadside sex workers. Truckstop prostitution in India is a dangerous business, and the women must be tough. *Murshidabad District, West Bengal, India.* ACHINTO

125

are absent, and those who 'talk bad' to the women are greeted by the drivers with disapproving silence.

Kabita sends her son down the road for plates of *dido*—a thick paste of corn or wheat that is eaten with lentils and curry—common fare in the hills of Nepal. The plates are brought by a 40-year-old woman who talks to Kabita with great animation. She wears a small, tight *choli* blouse and a colourful sash round her waist, the garb of a hill sex worker of a few years ago.

After she leaves, the driver confides, 'Now, just a few of her old lovers come, pay her 50 rupees a time. But she has her *dhaba*, she sells local spirits, makes her *dido*.' For a moment, at his comment, Kabita's eyes flash hard once again, perhaps looking into the future.

Kabita is nearing the end of her profession. Although reluctant to discuss her plans, she is thinking of her children and herself a few years from now. Two months ago, she rented this *dhaba*, and if all goes well, she may expand.

Some miles down the road towards the border, an older lady she knows has a *dhaba*, but business was not good. So she brought in a very lovely girl from Manipur, in eastern India. 'This is my younger sister,' she said. Since the girl arrived, business has been booming. One can tell by the number of trucks parked there in the evening. Whenever there are lots of trucks, Kabita says, there's a new girl in town. The Manipuri girl charges a lot, 500 rupees, more than twice the going rate. The entrepreneur

has a new radio, a new refrigerator. It is business, only business. We must take care of our children.

'I don't know,' Kabita says. 'I want to go to "Arab". I have two, three brothers there. My in-laws are there. I can make a lot of money. They said they'll make my passport and visa and ticket. I'll go to "Arab" and earn. I don't know what the work will be. My parents will take care of my children. I have a little land; they can get something from the land while I'm gone. I don't know.'

Again, her eyes harden. One can feel years of unpleasant memories behind her eyes.

'I want to go, but I can't because of the kids. I want to send them to boarding school. I don't know.'

Although Kabita is virtually illiterate, her mind is brilliant. She adds long tariff bills in her head and remembers conversations verbatim she'd had months before. She is very active in the programmes of the local HIV/AIDS intervention organisation, taking a central part in meetings of roadside sex workers. She is aware of the risk of HIV infection, aware that the truckstops are among the highest risk for any sex worker in the country.

'Kabita took an STD test,' a local health outreach worker says. 'But she refuses to have an AIDS test. What good would it do? It would only destroy her mind.'

Kabita shakes her head quickly, as if to shake ghosts from her hair, and the smile comes back into her eyes. She empties her glass, fills the other glasses, then fills her own. 'Can I have a cigarette?,' she asks. 'Ah yes,' she sighs, resting her head on her driver's shoulder. 'Tomorrow I'll go to Mugling.'

Street sex workers and truckstop sex workers share many of the same problems, including a high risk of HIV infection and little protection from abuse by police and clients. *Ramna Park, Dhaka, Bangladesh.* MAHMUD

BY JOHN FREDERICK

PHOTOGRAPHS BY MANI LAMA, ACHINTO AND MAHMUD

CONDOMS ON THE ROAD
General Welfare Pratisthan
Halting Aids on the Highways

'First we talk about other things, maybe the weather, maybe the harvest, sometimes we talk about the heroes and heroines of the films,' says Mahesh Bhattarai. 'After some time, we slip into the real issue. This is a very personal issue, a stigmatised issue. We can't just shake their hands and start talking about sex.'

Mahesh is the Director of General Welfare Pratisthan (GWP), a Nepali NGO that conducts HIV/AIDS interventions for truckdrivers and sex workers along 450 kilometres of Nepal's highways, from Kathmandu to the Indian border.

'It is difficult to catch a truckdriver in India,' says Atanu Majumdar, 'Nepal is very small, but in India the distances are so great.' Atanu is Project Manager of Halting AIDS on the Highways (HAH), the Indian half of the highway intervention equation. HAH is supported by Bhoruka Welfare Trust, a social service organisation of the Transport Corporation of India. The project operates a web of intervention centres stretching from Nepal to the Bangladesh border, reaching north into Assam and halfway down the long coast of India to Andhra Pradesh.

Truckdrivers are promiscuous. On the road for weeks or months, with a wife in a distant village, a cowboy bravado, and little else but the highway for entertainment, drivers likely attend prostitutes—and transmit HIV—more often than any other type of client.

Each NGO uses different strategies for different highways and different styles of the sex trade. Nepal's truckstops are smaller, more 'homely', and GWP can use students, villagers, truckers and the sex workers themselves to deliver safe-sex messages and condoms.

'The sex workers are shy to come out,' says GWP's Mahesh, 'so we ask them to come to a picnic spot at a river bank or park. We dance and sing and cook food, and slowly we come to the issue.' With the drivers, GWP outreach workers catch the men at their eating places or just hop in the truck.

'In India, most highway sex workers live in nearby settlements,' says HAH's Atanu, 'so to reach them anonymously, we have outreach clinics which address the whole community around the truckstop. The roads here are so long, so to catch the truckdrivers we set up visiting centres where they can relax and watch TV. There we have STD services and counselors for AIDS awareness.'

Both NGOs support their personal contact by holding STD camps and awareness activities such as films and street theatre, and each supports the other. GWP sends their street theatre troupes across the border to perform for Indian truckdrivers. In turn, HAH reciprocates with medical personnel for the STD camps.

For truckdrivers, sex workers or for anyone, sex is a very personal matter—and a safe-sex message will only stick if it is non-judgemental. 'We don't say sex work is right or wrong,' says Mahesh. 'We just try to develop relationships.

— JF

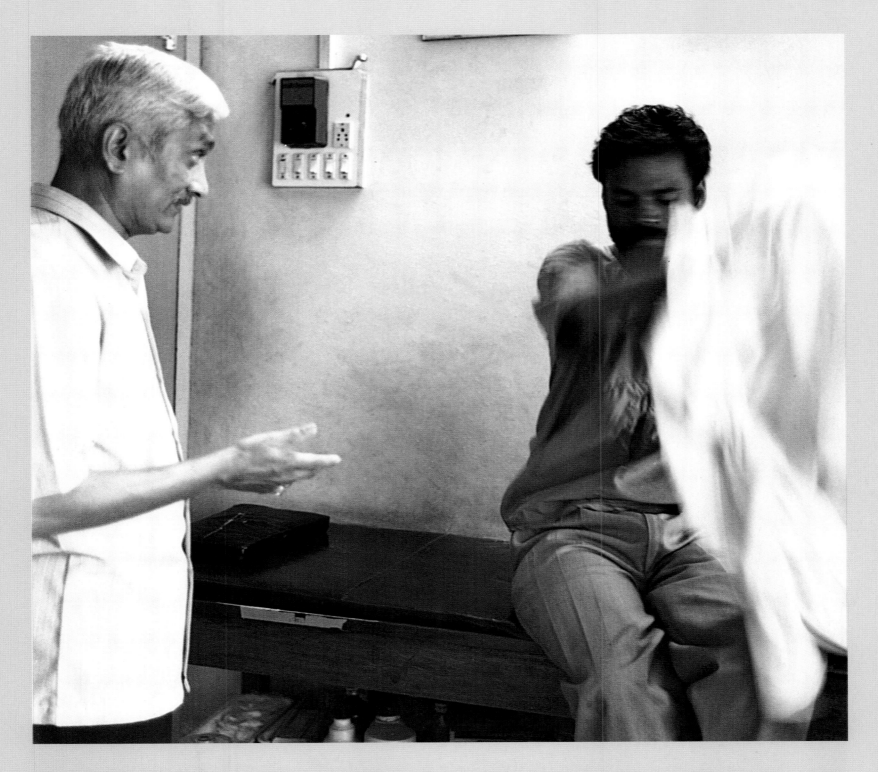

An HIV–positive truckdriver is examined by a doctor at a roadside STD/HIV clinic. *West Bengal, India*. Thomas L. Kelly

DANGEROUS LIAISONS

Girish

Girish denies that he is a 'sex worker'. He has sex with men, and they usually pay him for it. He does not regard it as a job, much less a profession. It is simply what he does, while he waits for alternative employment. The fact that sex with men has proved lucrative for him does not make his occupation a significant source of identity. Neither does his sexual orientation. He knows the word 'gay', but does not recognise himself in the term. It is certainly not a major determinant of his sense of self. What happened to him was, he insists, beyond his will.

Girish is tall and slim, with pale skin, very dark eyes and a mass of black hair that falls over his forehead. He is elegant, dressed in tight jeans and boots, with a loose acid-green shirt.

Born in a village in Uttar Pradesh some 70 kilometres from Kanpur, he is the eldest of three brothers and two sisters. His parents had a small plot of land, but this was forfeited to a moneylender when Girish was about six. Girish came with his father to Delhi in 1986, when he was 10. The biggest city he had seen was the neighbouring market-town.

'I looked out at the traffic, all the people. I felt happy. I would get a proper wage, I told myself, I would send money home. I thought of my mother's face when I went home and opened up my wallet, hundreds of rupees. You know, a 100-rupee note at home was a lot of money.

A male sex worker and his client in the 'jungle' of a large urban park. *New Delhi, India.* ANITA KHEMKA

'The only work for my father was to hire a cycle rickshaw. You had to pay rent—25 rupees a day—to the owner, and then the rest was yours. But it was very hard. My father worked so many hours, the others said to him, "You won't last two years." But he said "Just two years, then we'll go home and buy some land."

'One day, I went to Connaught Place with some of the boys from Gole Market where we were living. That was where my eyes were opened. In the evening, many men came into the Central Park (the rotunda at the heart of Connaught Place). They were looking for sex. At that time, the bushes were quite thick, there were places to hide. In parts of the park there were no lights. Some of the shoe-shine boys knew they could make money by going with these men. One boy showed me 500 rupees he had been given. I was frightened, but at the same time, I wanted to know about this thing. For a long time, I did nothing. Sometimes I would just stay there, in the shadows, watching to see what would happen.

'When I was 13, I was picked up by a man. He might have been the same age as my father, 40. He took me into the bushes. It was late in the night, about ten o'clock. He put his penis between my legs and kept on until he finished. Then he went away. And he didn't give me anything. I didn't tell anyone. I felt shame. I also felt foolish, because I had let him do this. I didn't really understand what it meant.

'My father was coughing all the time. He was sick. I told him he should go home. He didn't want to, but he was so bad, you could see his bones through his skin. I bought a train ticket and went with him to the station. That was the last time I saw him. About a year later, a man from near our village came to Delhi to tell me my father was dead.

'I was alone in Delhi. I worked at the rickshaw for a little while. There wasn't much money. It was May. It was hot. Then I remembered what the boys had told me, and the man who had done sex with me. I thought maybe there was more money to be made like that. I was not really ready to do it, and I felt shame. But I thought I would try.

'The first man who picked me up had a Maruti in the Parking just outside the Central Park. He was not young, but he seemed kind. He took me to his house, in a posh colony in South Delhi. His wife was away. He gave me whisky, which I had never tasted. I didn't like it, but it helped, because when you take *sharab*, your mind is no longer connected to your body.

'I was very stupid, I did not know what to expect. He wanted to penetrate me. I didn't know such things were possible. I thought you just played with each other until you came. I wouldn't let him enter me. He became very angry. I didn't understand. He took me back to the Ring Road to wait for a bus and gave me 200 rupees. It was more money than I had earned in a day, but I knew it was nothing to what some of the boys got.

'I asked them, and they told me about penetration. I said I wasn't going to do that. I was still driving the rickshaw. It was hot. Finally, I thought, "Well, if this is what I have to do, I'll do it." So the next night I went

Kusal and Gopal have been intimate friends since their school days. Kusal has not spoken with his father for three years, after an argument about his sexual activities. Gopal keeps his relationship hidden from his family. *New Delhi, India.* ANITA KHEMKA

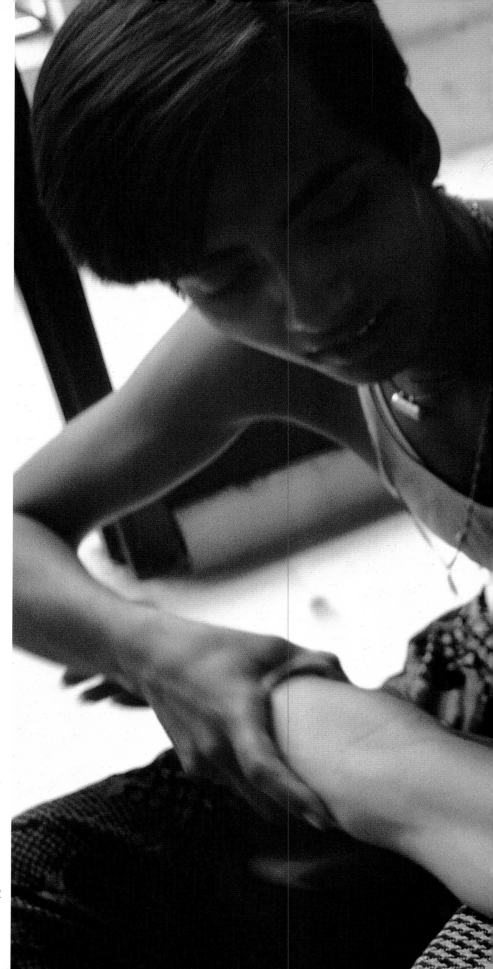

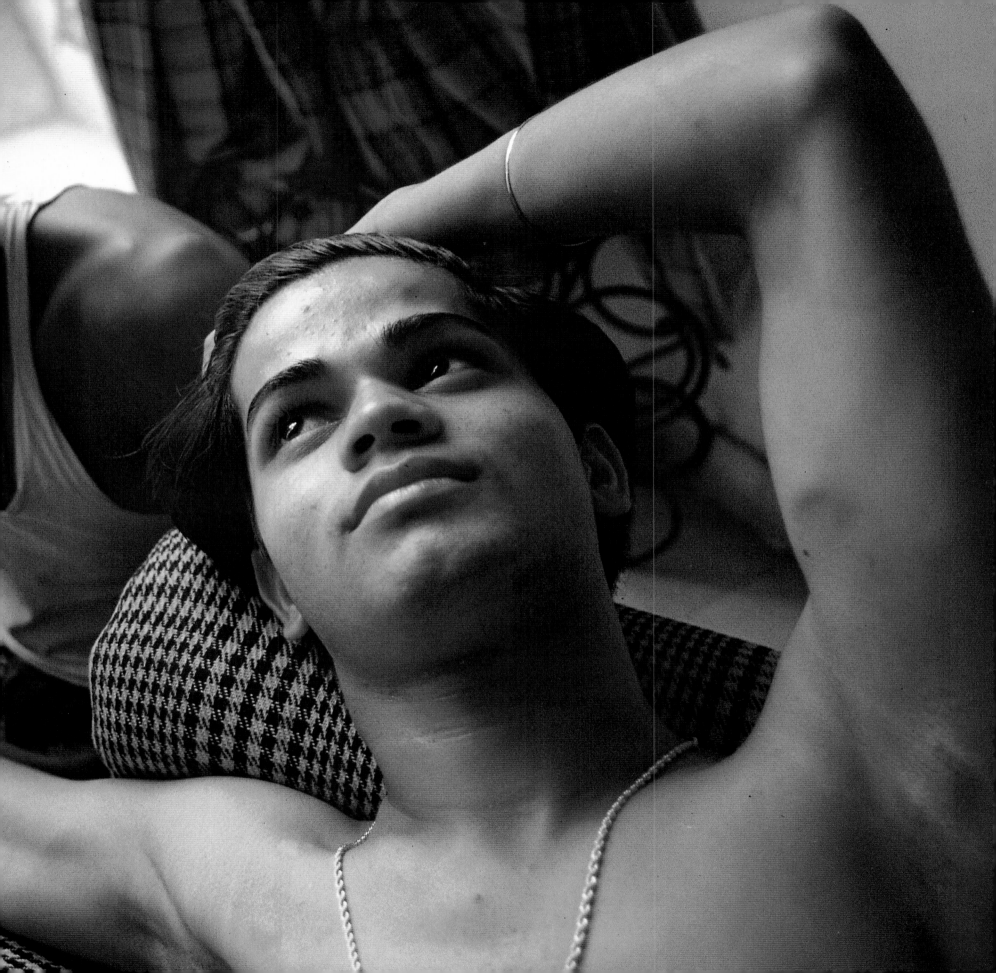

back to the Central Park. This man—he was quite old, about 50—wanted me to suck him. I didn't want to, but before I knew it, we were doing it in a dark part of the park. I was nearly sick. But he gave me 500 rupees. I had never seen so much money in my life. The thing had not taken more than five minutes.

'Some of the professionals told me, it isn't good to come every day to this place. The police get to know you. They told me that there are many places to go in Delhi, and you will not be seen all the time in the same locality. That is how I learned about Dhaula Kuan.'

Dhaula Kuan is on one of the main highways into Delhi, a large intersection and an interstate bus stop. It is always crowded and noisy; people with cases, bags and trunks; a jumble of trucks, buses, cars, taxis, auto-rickshaws, bicycles. Behind this is a large area of park and scrubland. Just inside the gate, flowerbeds give way to rocky pathways, a stretch of glassy, dark water, and then 'jungle'.

This is a major meeting place for men who have sex with men in Delhi. Close to the Cantonment area, there are men from the military and the police. There are a number of five-star hotels nearby, so hotel workers are well represented. There is usually a sprinkling of male government officials. They meet garment workers, migrant labourers, construction workers, shop workers. This population attracts many male sex workers, as well as some opportunists, blackmailers and robbers.

The most successful sex workers do not show any particular urgency about picking up clients, especially

Jacob (right), a social worker with male and transsexual prostitutes, relaxes with a transsexual *ali* friend at a local festival. *Villapuram, Chennai, India.* THOMAS L. KELLY

during the daytime. Sunday is the exception. This is a day off for most workers, and the park is always more crowded. The men pair off and disappear into the maze of pathways in the dense vegetation. The *khotis*, that is, men who are penetrated, are often cheated by the men who use them. They may be offered a derisory amount or nothing at all. Those who are young and attractive, however, are in demand. Many of these, including Girish, who is now very accomplished, can state their price and make good money.

It is into this environment that Girish came at the age of 16. He had to overcome his distaste for being penetrated, and now admits he doesn't care. Although he doesn't say he enjoys it, he knows it as a necessary part of the work that will earn him the considerable sums he can make.

Some of the men—the *giriyas*, as they are called by the *khotis*—have a regular partner. Not a relationship, not a friendship, but they return to the same boy again and again. Between the age of 16 and 20, Girish was earning several hundred rupees a day. He moved into a rented room in a building, and now has a small apartment in a house in Moti Bagh. He can easily afford the 4,000 rupees (US$ 90) a month.

'I know it's dangerous. We are sometimes picked up by the police. They will take money from us, beat us, and then sometimes have sex with us. They are our enemy. Most of the clients are okay. I don't do anything for less than 100 rupees, but I don't always get it. I have come to know all the cruising places in Delhi. I know which toilets to go to late at night, I know the parks, the temples, the mosques, the bus stands, and I go there on certain nights when there will be a crowd.

'There are many risks in what I do. I have more than once had an infection in the backside. There is a clinic which deals with such things. They gave me medicine and it went away. I know about AIDS. I also know that it doesn't happen overnight, but being poor happens all the time. I always carry condoms, and I ask the men to use them. Sometimes they do. But if I tell them they might catch something, they will think I have some disease. And if they refuse to use it, if I'm hungry, I'll let them go ahead anyway.

'I've never had sex with a woman. Some of the men are kind to me. They are like my father. But I do not kiss. I like to go to sleep in a bed, with somebody's arms around me. Then I feel good.

'In Delhi, everything is secret. Most of the men are married, they have families. If anyone talks about these things they will say it is a disgrace, it is un-Indian, it should be stopped. But they still come on Sundays or holidays. Most of them feel shame. After they have finished they are generally in a bad mood and angry with you. Sometimes they may beat you; you can feel their hatred, because you are what they want, and they are ashamed.

'The boys have no bargaining power, because there are more of them than there are men willing to pay. This is why you have to accept anyone who approaches you. It doesn't matter if he is old, whether he is Hindu or Muslim, whether you like him or not.

'I send money home. Sometimes 1,000 a month, sometimes 2,000. They have begun to rebuild our house. My mother believes that I am working in a hotel. I went home last year. I took clothes and presents for my brothers and sisters. They think I am successful. They cannot imagine that such things happen.

'I would like to stop, but I cannot do anything else. Also, I am hooked. Sex is like brown sugar, it's addictive. My day is always the same, but it is always different,

A male sex worker (standing) solicits a client at an outdoor restaurant. *Karachi, Pakistan.* THOMAS L. KELLY

because I never know who I might meet. I get up late, make some breakfast, sit and watch TV, then have a bath and go out in the afternoon. Then after dark, I roam around the city. Go to sleep at twelve or one o'clock. I don't bring people to my rooms. I have good friends, but only in the park. In Dhaula Kuan, you can be yourself. When you come out of that place, you have to behave in a different way, you walk differently, you don't draw attention to yourself. This is Delhi.

'What is gay, I do not know. I do not enjoy. Most of the clients, all they want is release; *jaldi, jaldi* sex, come and go. They talk of love, but they mean sex. I would like to have someone who cares for me. I think I like women. I will get married, but not until I am 30 or maybe more. I cannot go back home. I would like to start a business, but I don't save any money. Maybe when I am too old, I will get a job.'

Girish with his fine figure, tight jeans, dark hair almost blue-black, teeth—a sliver of new moon between dark crimson lips, is probably at the peak of his earning power. He knows each day he runs the risk of infection, violence, humiliation. He doesn't think of it. Livelihood is paramount, even when it is at war with life itself.

BY JEREMY SEABROOK
PHOTOGRAPHS BY ANITA KHEMKA
AND THOMAS L. KELLY

137

ADDRESSING OTHER SEXUALITIES
The Naz Foundation (India) Trust

Male-to-male sex is prevalent throughout South Asia, but, as in the West 40 years ago, it is concealed by those who practise it and denied by the public and governments. 'Sometimes, I don't know if people are even aware of what's around them. Definitely they're not talking about it,' says Anjali Gopalan, Executive Director of the Naz Foundation (India) Trust in New Delhi. Naz is one of a handful of organisations in South Asia dedicated to raising awareness of HIV/AIDS and sexual health among people of all sexual orientations, including males who have sex with males (MSMs).

The issue of HIV transmission between males is only beginning to appear on donor agendas and government plans of action. UNAIDS estimates that at least 5% to 10% of all HIV cases worldwide are due to sexual transmission between males. The percentage in South Asia, however, is still unknown.

In South Asia, HIV interventionists are confronted with a challenging paradox. At a societal level, male-to-male sex is stigmatised—but at a personal level, it is often not considered unusual or 'abnormal'. Many MSMs do not identify themselves as 'gay', and often lead 'normal' lives as husbands and fathers. This paradox is compounded—and further confused—by the region's powerful male-female gender stereotypes and by the society's great reluctance to discuss sexual issues.

For Naz, the first step is to clear the air—to educate the public about sexuality, sexual health and HIV/AIDS.

The NGO conducts training for school students, teachers, NGO workers and medical personnel, among others, and encourages the government and donor organisations to include male-to-male sexual activity on the agendas of HIV intervention.

On the ground, however, almost all male-to-male sexual activity is secretive and conducted in an atmosphere of guilt and denial. For fear of censure, few MSMs visit reputable clinics if they have a sexual disease, and few physicians are either aware of or inclined to investigate anal or oral sexually transmitted diseases (STDs). In response, Naz has opened information and support helplines, offers clinical and counseling care for those living with STDs or HIV, and conducts sexual health programmes for both men and women.

Outreach workers, many of whom are MSMs, contact men and boys in parks and public places, to talk about HIV/AIDS and safe sex. Regular support group meetings of MSMs and male sex workers are held so they can share their problems of family, marriage pressures and peer relationships, discuss solutions, and begin the process of self-identity, which Naz thinks is essential to the adoption of safe-sex practices. 'The community itself', says Anjali, 'has to take a stand and say: "Okay, this is who we are and this is what we are—we're not strange creatures from another planet"—as most of society still thinks they are.'

— JF

138

Boys get ready for a party held by the Naz Foundation, in which sex workers gather for mutual support. Going to the party dressed as women, they fill up water balloons to pad their brassieres. *New Delhi, India*. ANITA KHEMKA

6

In the Name of God

Religion and Prostitution

In South Asia, as elsewhere, prostitution and religion have been bed-fellows throughout history. Gatherings of the faithful are gatherings of potential clients. Sex workers are found near all the major temple sites and pilgrimage places, and show up for business at all religious festivals.

Religion plays a significant role in legitimating the sexual abuse and prostitution of lower-caste and tribal women, who make up the majority of sex workers in South Asia. Basic Hindu and Buddhist tenets reinforce the caste and class hierarchy—the wealthy are wealthy because of their virtuous actions in their last birth. All of the major South Asian religions strongly reinforce patriarchal gender roles in their social teachings, if not in the habits of their deities. Both Hindu and Buddhist tantric texts specifically recommend sex with lower-caste women as one of the worldly vehicles to liberation.

To soften the shame of sex work and ease the pain of social ostracism, tribal sex worker communities often create myths of their downfall from a noble status in ancient times or of their curse to forever work as 'entertainers' after having slighted a god.

In many parts of Hindu South Asia, children are dedicated to the ritual service of a temple deity. 'Married' to the deity, the 'sacred servants' cannot take a human spouse, and many live off the earnings of prostitution. In some cases, as in the *deuki* system of Western Nepal, poor children are purchased by prosperous families and offered to temples in exchange for the deity's boon of more prosperity. Other systems, as among the Jogins of Andhra Pradesh, are more directly exploitative—here, a wealthy man may pay the family for a girl's dedication and the right to her virginity. Poor families are thankful to be relieved of a daughter's dowry burden, and in some cases have expectations of living off her earnings as a sex worker. Today, as in the *devadasi* system of Karnataka, dedication of children has become part of the established sex industry, and agents seek out the families to purchase dedicated girls to fill town and city brothels.

While the region is unique for the elaborate ways in which religion has been used to legitimate prostitution, it is also unique for religion's great tolerance of the profession. In South Asia, unlike the West, sex workers have seldom been the victims of holy self-righteousness.

— JOHN FREDERICK

Three generations of *deuki*. In the *deuki* system of Nepal, children are dedicated as servants to temple deities. Forbidden to marry, many support themselves by prostitution. Their illegitimate daughters usually follow in their mothers' profession. *Far Western Region, Nepal.* THOMAS L. KELLY

Many of the children
dedicated as servants to
Goddess Yellama end up in
urban brothels. *Devadasis* pay
homage to the Goddess at
their brothel shrine.
Kamathipura, Mumbai.
THOMAS L. KELLY

Religion and Prostitution

HANDMAIDEN OF THE GODDESS

Lalita

INDIA

Perched on her mother's shoulder, her eyelashes and matted dreadlocks drenched in fluorescent yellow turmeric, eight-year-old Lalita maintains a surprising calm amidst the frenzy that surrounds her. Thousands of women are weeping, trembling in trance, eyes rolling, speaking rapidly in tongues, while others faint and collapse. The ecstatic pounding of drums and the devotional roar of 300,000 pilgrims is deafening. It is the January full moon at the temple of the goddess Yellama in Karnataka, India. Despite a legal ban, thousands of devout pilgrims, almost all of them low-caste farmers, have come to the festival to dedicate their daughters to the Goddess.

'We have brought Lalita here to dedicate her to Yellama,' her mother whispers, frightened by the police presence in the temple grounds. With telltale dreadlocks, and marriage beads of red and white, over 5,000 girls under 12 years of age have come to ritually 'marry' the Goddess in an ancient rite that some believe is more of a curse than a blessing.

After this day, Lalita will be known as a *devadasi*—a slave or servant of the Mother—and following the dictates of custom, will not be entitled to marry. Like many of the *devadasis* in Karnataka, Lalita will likely become a prostitute.

'It is the Goddess's wish that Lalita become a *devadasi*,' her mother explains. 'When her dreadlocks appeared, we knew it was a sign that she had been chosen by the Goddess. Lalita was very sick when she was young. I prayed to Yellama to help her and she got better. Lalita must serve Yellama—it is the Goddess's wish.'

Despite her mother's devotion to Yellama, many suspect it is often more the parents' wish than the Goddess's to see daughters dedicated. The followers of Yellama come from the lowest tier of a poor agricultural society—low-caste, bonded farm labourers who till the soil for their landlords. A *devadasi* does not require a dowry, which sends so many of the poor even deeper into debt. Many impoverished parents are paid by wealthy patrons to dedicate their daughters to Yellama, so that the patrons may receive a boon from the deity. Since marriage to Yellama ritually turns a daughter into a groom and a son, poor parents without sons dedicate their last daughter in the hope that she will provide for them in their old age.

According to the 1984 Devadasi Prohibition Act, dedication of girls as *devadasis* is illegal and unconstitutional in India. However, the act allows for the initiation of girls to serve divine beings as ritual functionaries provided it is 'sacred, noble in character,' and 'free from sex'.

This reflects an orthodox Hindu vision of the past, not the reality of today. Nine hundred years ago, revered as chaste virgins meant only for the gods, *devadasis* lived in the temples—not on the streets—and entertained Yellama daily with devotional songs and dances, ceremonially feeding, bathing and fanning her. Later, the *devadasis* became the most cultured and educated women in medieval India. No other women were allowed to read or write or to own property. Poets wrote love sonnets and kings bestowed estates on worldly, successful *devadasis*

Drenched in yellow turmeric powder, with images of goddess Yellama balanced on their heads, *devadasis* in trance weave through the crowds at the Yellama festival. *Saundatti, Karnataka, India.* THOMAS L. KELLY

who were famed for their skills in the art of dance, music, conversation, perfumery and love-making.

Controversy rages about how the original vestal virgins became temple courtesans. Some historians believe that kings, wealthy landlords and invading Muslims conquered the temples and forced beautiful, low-caste women to become mistresses and prostitutes. Others believe that kings placed the dancing prostitutes in the temples to attract more pilgrims and revenue. Indeed, temple records show that *devadasi* earnings from prostitution often helped to defray temple costs—in the 18th century kingdom of Vijayanagar, the entire police force was paid from the money earned by *devadasis*.

Historical evidence suggests that *devadasis* may never

have been chaste virgins: as sacred prostitutes, *devadasis* offered their bodies in the name of the Goddess to priests and pilgrims. Similar to ancient Egyptian temples dedicated to Isis and the Greek temples dedicated to Aphrodite and Dionysus, sexual union with dancing prostitutes was considered an essential temple sacrament, mimicking the coupling of earth and sky, ensuring the fertility of the fields. Though devotion to Yellama stays unwavering, sex for the modern-day *devadasi* is sheer economics: a way of survival.

Today, the temple no longer supports the ritual services of the *devadasis*. The government priests now feed, bathe and clothe the Goddess, performing duties once restricted to *devadasis*. They are officially banned from coming to the temple during festival time.

'They used to come to the festival and they'd fall into a trance and run around the temple, ripping their clothes off,' explains Isworappa, a newly-appointed government priest. 'It became such a spectacle that people came to watch them dance naked instead of worshipping the deity. It had to be stopped.'

'We come, despite the ban,' says Vidyappa, an elderly *devadasi*. 'But we can no longer dance before Yellama.'

Covered with turmeric dust, symbolic of Yellama's curative powers, crowds of turbaned villagers proudly carry village Yellama idols towards the temple, shouting 'Udheyo! Udheyo! Rise up to the Mother!' Women wave ceremonial yak tails, a vestige of their heritage as temple courtesans. The full moon and the camphor torches reveal a snaking line of devotees waiting eagerly for a glimpse of the 600-year-old, black-faced stone idol housed in the inner sanctum of the temple. Outside, women dance wildly to the pulse of the village drums as they experience the force of Yellama's spirit rising within them.

In ancient times, the *devadasis'* seductive dancing enticed the dry heavens to pour life-giving water on the earth. It is no coincidence that Yellama's full moon festival occurs exactly one month before harvest. *Devadasis* still carry the waterpot on their heads as symbols of the Mother Goddess's power to seduce the Male Sky God. According to traditional Hindu texts, women have four times the sexual power of men and are four times as unable to resist the sexual urge. The male orthodox priests dismiss the village women and their ecstatic display of folk devotion.

'It is all drama—those village women in trance,' says the government priest. 'It is not the *shakti* of the Goddess as they claim. They do it for money. They think the Goddess is dwelling within them. But it is all fake.'

'Yellama first came to me ten years ago,' old Vidyappa says. 'I entered the temple courtyard and suddenly felt a great heat rising from the ground and travelling through my body. I collapsed. I lost consciousness. All I saw was white light. When I woke I felt cleansed and purified and knew I had to devote myself to Yellama or I would become very sick.'

Now that dedication has been banned, Lalita's parents and fellow villagers carry her around the temple before returning to their camp outside the grounds. 'I bathed and was anointed with oil,' says Lalita. 'I walked around the temple three times. We brought gifts for the priest. Then he tied a string around a statue of Yellama and then around me. He gave me a bamboo basket to carry on my head and a *chowdike* (a one-stringed musical instrument used for singing when collecting alms).'

'Some of the priests continue to perform the ceremony, only now because of the ban they do it in secret and charge more money,' complains Lalita's mother.

In ancient times, *devadasis* were meant to be consorts of the gods. The king, as a mortal divinity, was the only

145

man who could sleep with a *devadasi*. It was his duty to sponsor her puberty ceremony and deflower her before she went to the temple. Times have changed and on reaching puberty, Lalita may be given to a patron—usually a richer, upper-caste man—who will sponsor her ceremony. After the village feast, he will make love to her and can use her sexually for as long as he pleases.

Almost a third of the women dedicated to Yellama end up in the red-light districts of Mumbai, Pune or Gokak—breeding grounds for HIV/AIDS. The HIV rate among commercial sex workers in these cities is amongst the highest in South Asia, nearly 50 per cent. A few *devadasis* working in Mumbai make a point of travelling to the festival in hopes that Yellama will cure them of their sexually transmitted diseases.

Suvarna has come from Bhandup, a shanty town suburb of Mumbai, to pay obeisance to Yellama at her yearly festival. Were she not thin and sad-eyed, she would be almost comical in her faded sari covered in bright yellow turmeric.

'See these discolored patches on my gums?' she asks, opening her mouth wide. 'A sign from Yellama. My parents dedicated me because of this.

'There were four brothers and four sisters in my family, too many children. I worked in the sugarcane and cotton fields near my village. My parents encouraged me to go to town and work as a prostitute to earn money for the family. I would go to weekly fairs and cinema houses, and sometimes bring clients home. One day, my uncle invited an agent to our home from a nearby town. He gave my family some money and I went with him. He

Each year in January, thousands of poor, low-caste farmers go on pilgrimage to the temple of Goddess Yellama for her annual festival. *Saundatti, Karnataka, India.* THOMAS L. KELLY

took me to Mumbai and sold me to one of the brothels.

'There were many *devadasis* in Mumbai. Some of them were ashamed of their dreadlocks and would cut them. They all died. If you cut your dreadlocks, you cut your vow to Yellama and she gets revenge. I just have a small dreadlock—I used to hide it under my loose hair so the clients wouldn't see it.

'Our madam was a *devadasi* and kept a shrine in the brothel. We would worship Yellama every day. She protects us from disease and from the evil eye— many people are jealous of prostitutes because we have jewellery, clothes and beauty. Now I'm old and I must survive by begging. I have come to the festival to beg.'

While many *devadasis* end up as prostitutes in towns and cities, most stay in the villages, often combining field work and prostitution. Lalita, like all *devadasis* in Karnataka, is a *dalit*—a low-caste bonded labourer.

'Lalita will not become a prostitute,' her mother says, 'It is only the bad *devadasis* who go to Mumbai and sell their bodies. Lalita will be different. She will come home with us. Her aunt, an old *devadasi*, will teach her how to propitiate Yellama in the village.'

Nearly two thirds of India's prostitutes come from the lower castes and tribes. Lalita's family, like many of the *dalits* of the subcontinent, has spent generations in debt

A *devadasi* in trance dances at the yearly festival to Yellama. She wears the distinctive dreadlocks and cowry shell necklace of the *devadasis*. *Saundatti, Karnataka.*
THOMAS L. KELLY

Facing page: A terrified child, about to be dedicated to the Goddess. Each year, an estimated 3,000 young girls are brought to the festival of Yellama to be dedicated as *devadasis*, or 'handmaidens of the Goddess'. *Saundatti, Karnataka.*
THOMAS L. KELLY

bondage to higher-caste landowners. Their future is written: either remain in bondage, with another's land to till for a small share of the grain, or seek their 'freedom', with no land to till and no grain to feed the family. None dare choose the latter.

'After Lalita menstruates, we will perform a big ceremony. She will have a ritual bath, a new sari, and will go to the village well and carry holy water in a pot to the Yellama shrine at our home. Then we will have a big community feast.'

Her mother pauses, looking out at the milling throng of ragged villagers. 'After that, she may go to find work in the cities.'

BY V. CARROLL DUNHAM
PHOTOGRAPHS BY THOMAS L. KELLY

A former *devadasi*, now a project worker for the Devadasi Rehabilitation Project, cuts the dreadlocks of a young *devadasi*, symbolising her rejection of the practice. *Saundatti, Karnataka, India.* THOMAS L. KELLY

RESISTING RELIGIOUS EXPLOITATION
The Devadasi Rehabilitation Project

In early December, on the chilly, full-moon day known locally as Randi Hunnime, an unusual ceremony was observed in 167 villages of Belgaum District in northern Karnataka, India. Rejecting an age-old custom of breaking bangles to observe a one-month period of 'widowhood' with Goddess Yellama before the January full moon festival, groups of former *devadasis* performed the ceremony in reverse—symbolising a break with the practice that has held them in bondage for the better part of their lives. The former *devadasis* wore their bangles proudly and publicly, while taking an oath rejecting the demeaning status and identity of the *devadasi*. They erected notice boards publicising their pledge, and led joyous processions around the villages.

With the assistance of the Devadasi Rehabilitation Project, operated by Myrada, a Karnataka-based NGO, and the Karnataka State Women's Development Corporation, the women have formed a campaign for the eradication of the *devadasi* system. The project is helping former *devadasis* achieve economic self-sufficiency through job training, loans and the provision of homes and house sites. Self-help groups have been established and encouraged to start rotating savings accounts in local banks. Most important, these groups have become platforms where the previously muted women can articulate their needs, their anger and their faith.

However, despite activists' progressive advancements, dedication of girls into the service of Yellama continues.

'It is our custom. It is a boon to be dedicated,' says Suvarna, a *devadasi* who spent years working in a Mumbai brothel. 'If we abandon this practice, we will be cursed. We are happy with this custom, it must be perpetuated. My daughter will not be a *devadasi*. But I had my younger sister and brother's daughter dedicated. They will take care of me when I am old.'

A thousand-year-old tradition is not eradicated overnight. In the eyes of many, including some conservative members of India's women's movement, the plight of the *devadasis* is exaggerated and the value of an ancient religious tradition outweighs the freedom of 'a few thousand women'. Likely, however, this tradition oppresses far more than 'a few thousand', and as awareness grows that the dedicated are mere children, too young to freely choose their future, the challenge to the *devadasi* system is certain to continue.

'I was dedicated at the age of 10, and in my eighteenth year became a "keep" to a man,' says Sitavva, a dark, round-faced woman of 25 from Kabbur village. 'Then he got married to a woman of his own caste and left me. I will not let my daughter be dedicated.'

'I don't have to be a concubine, a prostitute or a beggar to worship Yellama,' the elderly *devadasi* Moneeka declares. 'I can serve the Goddess without being a slave to society.'

—VCD

Anita, daughter of a prostitute, lives in a hostel for the children of sex workers. She is a good student and one of the best dancers in the hostel's dance troupe. *Calcutta.* ACHINTO

7

Let Us Be

Dignity, Protection and the Right to Work

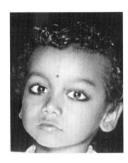

Throughout the world, the majority of adult female sex workers have children. The majority are at risk of HIV infection. The majority have been beaten, burned or raped. All will get old, and lose their clients to younger women. Almost none wanted to enter prostitution and almost none can leave it. Bound to their profession, prostitutes live and work, raise their children, pay their bills, fall ill—just like the rest of us.

And there they are, all over South Asia—perhaps millions of them—lurking on the street corners, peering out of windows, sitting at the corner tables of restaurants. They are a source of discomfort—their ubiquitous presence brings up righteous indignation, pity, lust and guilt in the public, the media and the boardrooms. And their numbers are growing.

What's to be done with all these fallen angels? Everybody has ideas, but nobody seems to come to any conclusions, even about the nature of the beast. This is greatly due to a semantic simplification—'sex work', like the word 'trafficking', is a single term signifying two vitally different concepts. A sharp line must be drawn between 'entering sex work' and 'living as a sex worker'.

On the former side of the line are the forms of physical, social and structural coercion—trafficking, marginalisation, child abuse, poverty, gender inequality,

male lust and power—and here, intolerance and abolition are operative terms. However, on the other side of that line are humans in the profession, unable to escape and doing the best they can—here, the operative terms are compassion, support, respect and equality.

It is unlikely that any South Asian government or the public will give full recognition to sex workers' needs for many years. However, some adjustments in the legal systems, some support and some curtailment of abuse—especially by the police—are taking place. And thus, the word 'legalisation' has again raised its hoary head. Today, the relevant debate is no longer between legalisation and criminalisation—the debate is between legalisation and decriminalisation. Unfortunately, in common parlance the word 'legalisation' embraces both of these quite discrete concepts—a semantic constraint like the terms 'sex work' and 'trafficking'—and this has thrown the debate into utter confusion.

To 'legalise' means to label prostitution as a special occupation, subject to regulation. As history has shown, regulation has invariably had dire consequences for sex workers—their workplaces have been 'ghettoised', they have been subject to enforced health checks, their children have been taken away 'for their own protection', and they have come under increased police control. This has hardly addressed their needs.

Decriminalisation, on the other hand, means 'let them

be'—take prostitution off the books, no more subject to special regulation than carpentry or accounting. Sex workers would enjoy the same civil liberties, working conditions and social benefits as other employed persons, and be protected by the same laws against violence, rape, child sexual abuse and child labour. By the same token, the profession would be subject to the same business standards, and sex workers would be accountable for the same proper care of their children.

Decriminalisation is a hard goal to achieve. For one, it puts the onus on governments to say that sex work is a legitimate occupation. For another, criminal networks which feed off the industry must still be controlled. The profession also needs special assistance. The public must be educated in order to change attitudes which stigmatise prostitutes and their children, and health programmes must still focus on the profession's high risk for STD and HIV transmission.

With decriminalisation, the forms of coercion which send people into sex work will have to be addressed with greater strength. The intent of decriminalisation is to support those already in the trade, not to support an industry that enriches itself by cultivating oppression. Thus, the client must be addressed—the guy who has walked free thus far, who has created the market for children, transmitted HIV with impunity, and generated a demand for sex so great that it has made slavery of the profession. And this puts the issue of sexuality directly in the faces of all South Asian people.

— JOHN FREDERICK

A sex worker roughs up a client who refused to pay the agreed-upon price. *Dhaka, Bangladesh.* SHEHZAD NOORANI

Dignity, Protection and Right to Work

PROFESSION, NOT OPPRESSION   Sex Workers of Calcutta

INDIA

In 1992, Dr Smarajit Jana, an epidemiologist with the All-India Institute of Hygiene and Public Health, was hired to conduct a three-month survey of Calcutta's brothels, collecting baseline information in preparation for an AIDS intervention programme. When the survey—still the most comprehensive in South Asia—was completed, Dr Jana was asked to stay on. He reluctantly accepted. Fortunately for Calcutta, Dr Jana was a man blessed with awareness of his own ignorance.

'The basic fact,' says Dr Jana, 'was that I was really ignorant about the whole sex trade and its practices. I tried to do some background research, but I soon realised that in order to learn something about this community, I had to open a dialogue with the sex workers.

'The more I opened the dialogue, the more I entered into a unique world. What intrigued me was the way they started communicating with me. The moment a sex worker accepts you as someone who will not create a problem, she shares her feelings, emotions, all those things. That helped me understand many, many other issues which one cannot see in the very limited domain of health care or HIV/STD intervention.

'I started to realise that the usual approaches would not be very effective. Providing AIDS awareness and condoms

isn't going to be successful because sex workers have no power compared to the clients, the pimps or the madams. Without strengthening them, you cannot change this power equation.

'The first step was to create an enabling environment, beginning with some sort of social support service like a water or electricity connection to a red-light district or a clinic for sex workers. It's a sort of recognition by the "authorities" to make them understand that they are accepted as human beings.'

With a small clinic set up in a men's club in the old brothel district of Sonagachi, the STD/HIV Intervention Programme (SHIP)—and the empowerment of Calcutta's sex workers—began. Along with the clinic and an information component, a primary feature of the programme was condom distribution and HIV awareness through 'peer educators'—sex workers who would carry the latex and the safe-sex messages to other sex workers.

The modus operandi of the project was distilled to three words: Reliance, Respect and Recognition. In programme design, reliance would be placed on the sex workers' understanding of their own needs, they would be respected as human beings, and their profession would be recognised as a valid means of supporting themselves and their children.

The project was to be guided by the needs expressed by the sex workers. As the peer educators made their rounds of the brothels and listened to the concerns of

During 'sit and draw' days organised by the Mahila Samanwaya Committee, the children of sex workers gather to play with paper and crayons. This is the first time that some of these children have ever picked up a crayon. *Sonagachi, Calcutta.* THOMAS L. KELLY

their 'sisters', expression soon came forth. Says Dr Debasis Bose, physician with SHIP, 'They could not make up the peer education reports; they went to seminars but could not read the transparencies. Education was a need of the community. They told us, "We cannot participate because we can't read. Either educate us or don't send us anywhere."'

So a literacy programme was created for the peer educators. After they finished their rounds of the brothels, they sat in the courtyard outside the clinic, studying their ABCs with a primer which they themselves had designed with a local educator. Soon they expressed their need for training on their legal rights, and this was provided by volunteer lawyers.

The growth of their self-confidence and their concern about police harassment led to their expression of a very important need: an organisation of their own which would address not only health problems, but all their concerns.

In 1995, they created the first collective of sex workers in South Asia: the Durbar Mahila Samanwaya Committee (DMSC). 'Some of our major problems were frequent police raids, conflicts with the clients and extortion of money by the local thugs,' says Mala Singh, the present Secretary of the DMSC.

It is appropriate that South Asia's first sex worker organisation should have been started in Calcutta, a city of intellect, radical thought and unionisation. The Committee's first major public presentation was dramatic—1,000 sex workers gathered in a massive demonstration before a local police station to protest

Members of the Durbar Mahila Samanwaya Committee gather in a May Day rally in support of the sex workers of Rajabazar Brothel. *Medinipore, West Bengal.* ACHINTO

police raids in the Sonagachi brothel district. Not surprisingly, as Mala says, 'Immediately, the intensity of police harassment declined.' From the beginning, however, they have tried to work out their problems by peaceful discussion. 'In matters like this,' says Mala, 'negotiation is best.'

After a difficult time getting support from the pimps, the DMSC began to mediate in disputes with the clients, and the sex workers increasingly gained power behind the brothel curtains. 'What has happened,' says Dr Jana, 'is that recently not only their clients, but even their long-time lovers are apprehensive about the name of the Mahila Samanwaya Committee. Now disputes are no longer mediated by the men's clubs and other men's groups; they go to the DMSC.'

Extortion of money by the thugs was a problem—but a relatively small problem compared to paying the bills, especially after they paid their percentages to the pimps and madams. Many stayed in perpetual debt to moneylenders, for loans borrowed at the exorbitant rate of 2 per cent a day. Saving for the future or paying for children's education was impossible. In 1995, they started the Usha Co-operative Multipurpose Society.

'We now have 600 members,' says Saraswati Sarkar, Secretary of the co-operative. 'Each member puts some small savings in the co-operative fund. Those who need can take loans at a reasonable interest. We need to save. We are concerned with the welfare of our children and the old sex workers.'

Today, in order to supplement their income, the women sew garments and knit sweaters to be sold through the co-operative. In co-ordination with SHIP, a social marketing programme on condoms is underway, and sex workers earn money from the sale of condoms in vast red-light markets such as Sonagachi.

After addressing the pressures of harassment and immediate economic security, the sex workers voiced strong concern for the welfare of their children. The Usha Co-operative started night crèches to care for infants while their mothers worked. To open up the world for young children confined to the brothels, 'sit and draw' days were routinely organised, in which mothers brought their children for group play with paper and crayons.

The women have rejected the idea of establishing a special school for their children—they are already ostracised, they say. To ensure that their children will be able to integrate into society, they want to send them to boarding schools or hostels, where they will have less contact with the red-light areas.

'Sex workers have become so conscious,' says project worker Mitra Routh, 'that they don't want their daughters to enter the profession. They say, "Let them be educated first. We are uneducated and illiterate, and we don't want our daughters to be marked as illiterate." '

Now, they address the needs of their daughters at the same time they address their own educational needs. Older girls are taking part in a new programme in which sex workers teach literacy skills to their peers, and are teaching the ABCs to their mothers and their 'aunties'.

To strengthen the self-esteem of sex workers and their children, the DMSC formed Komal Gandhar, a cultural troupe which showcases the talents of their community. Composed of male and female sex workers and their children, the troupe performs songs, dances and dramas, many of which tell of their lives in the brothels and their concerns about AIDS.

In the past few years, the DMSC has moved far beyond Calcutta's brothels. 'At present, we are in contact with 30,000 sex workers all over West Bengal,' says Mala Singh. 'Our members move from village to village and establish rapport with the people there. We are all sisters in the same boat.' DMSC members not only support fellow sex workers, they meet with police and administrators in rural areas and are opening up Health Care and Education Centres throughout the state.

The DMSC's outreach does not stop with sex workers. In 1996, they inaugurated West Bengal's first HIV-positive hotline. 'In West Bengal today,' says the physician Dr Bose, 'if somebody is HIV positive, they will be ostracised. Calls come from all over the state, and then a team goes there, talks with the patient and the family, and helps them work out their problems.'

In the past several years, DMSC leaders have travelled throughout India, making contacts with other sex worker groups in Delhi, Maharashtra and Tamil Nadu, and have travelled abroad to meet similar organisations and speak at conferences in the US, Europe and Southeast Asia.

The core members of the DMSC—perhaps 60 or 100 women, SHIP's original peer educators—recognise that with their power and awareness they are not representative of all the sex workers around them, an estimated 50,000 in Calcutta alone. But they also recognise that they do represent the voices of those on the ground. The DMSC's work is now two-fold: to respond to the immediate problems of their sisters and to bring their concerns to a national platform, and change existing laws that oppress them.

Says Mala Singh, 'We want the sex trade to be accepted as a profession just like any other, not labelled as something illegal. We want no special laws for sex workers, no issuing of identity cards, no restriction of working areas or other such forms of government regulation. All the laws of the land that are applicable to the rest of the citizens must also apply to us.'

While pushing for decriminalisation of those working

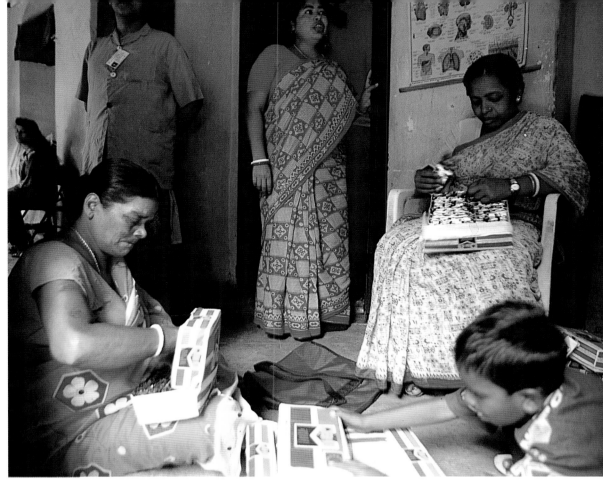

Sex workers and their children pack condoms in colourful boxes. Through their own social marketing programme, sex workers supplement their incomes by selling condoms in the busy brothel areas. *Sonagachi, Calcutta.* THOMAS L. KELLY

in the profession, the DMSC has taken a hard line on those who want to enter it. 'The Self-Regulatory Board,' says Mitra Routh, 'was formed by the sex workers, and includes government officials and members of India's Human Rights Commission. It prevents the entry of children and the unwilling entry of adult women.'

'The DMSC is taking active measures to stop child prostitution and trafficking,' says Mala Singh. 'We have identified traffickers and handed them over to the police. Many minor girls who were trafficked have been rescued and sent back home.'

'If a woman wants to enter prostitution in Sonagachi,' says Mitra, 'the Board finds out why she wants to come in, and if she has any other way of earning a living. If she has options, then she's sent to another profession suitable to her. Admission is allowed only if there is no other option.'

In 1999, SHIP and other external supporting organisations handed over the management of all project activities to the sex workers. The umbrella organisation, the Society for Human Development and Social Action, whose interim Project Director is the son of a sex worker, will now take the reins, from fundraising to accounting to mediating with the government. It is an immense challenge, but a challenge which signifies—at long last—that sex workers have some rights which they can exercise.

'A sex worker,' says Mala, 'should have the right to be a human being and should enjoy all the rights that a human being enjoys. Instead of abolishing the profession, the oppression and exploitation inherent in sex work should be abolished.'

BY JOHN FREDERICK
PHOTOGRAPHS BY THOMAS L. KELLY AND ACHINTO

Hotel workers taking a break on the beach. In Sri Lanka, female sex work is covert, and many women such as these use straight jobs as a cover for soliciting clients. *Colombo, Sri Lanka.* Thomas L. Kelly

CONTRIBUTORS

The Photographers

THOMAS L. KELLY came to Nepal in 1978 as a Peace Corps volunteer, and has since worked as a photo-activist, documenting the struggles of marginalised people and disappearing cultural traditions all over the world. Since the early 1990s, he has been recording the lives of sex workers and the traditions of prostitution across South Asia. Thomas has worked extensively for Unicef and Save the Children Fund (USA) on the subject of child prostitution, and his work on prostitution, trafficking and numerous other subjects has appeared in publications worldwide, including *National Geographic*, *Newsweek*, *Natural History*, *Smithsonian*, *Le Figaro*, *Stern* and *Geo*. Apart from photography, he has produced and directed films and videos on prostitution, violence against women, and esoteric ethnic practices, among other subjects. He has researched and photographed the books *Tibet: Reflections from the Wheel of Life*, *The Hidden Himalayas*, and *Kathmandu: City on the Edge of the World*, all published by Abbeville Press, NY. He was Associate Producer for the film *The Dragon Bride* for BBC and National Geographic magazine.

SHEHZAD NOORANI brings to this book nine years of experience photographing the lives of adult and child sex workers in India, Nepal, Thailand, the Philippines and his resident country, Bangladesh. His extensive documentation of sex work has appeared in *The New York Times*, *Asiaweek*, *Photographer's International*, *Internazionale* (Italy) and other publications. Shehzad's exhibitions include The Daughters of Darkness (on sex workers, Thailand, 1999), The Lives of People (on HIV/AIDS in developing countries, USA, 1998) and The Sexual Exploitation of Children (on child sexual abuse, Stockholm, 1996). Since 1987, Shehzad has worked as a freelance photographer and consultant with a special focus on social issues for numerous international organisations. His photographs have appeared in, among other publications, *In Harm's Way* and *Childhood Betrayed*, both published by Unicef.

MAHMUD has worked since 1992 as a documentary photographer in Bangladesh, working mostly with NGOs and donor agencies, including Unicef and UNDP. Also the Director of Map Photo Agency in Dhaka, Mahmud has created portfolios of portraits of Bangladeshi women, the gypsy community and sea-going fishermen, as well as photographic essays on the trafficking of Bangladeshi women and children.

MANI LAMA brought sex work to national attention in Nepal in 1995 with an exhibition of portraits of Nepali child prostitutes for Unicef. Since that time, he has photographed truck-stop prostitution, Tamang trafficking and the Badi and Deuki sex worker communities. His work has appeared in many international magazines, and he is the photographer of *Nepal: The Himalayan Kingdom* (Lustre Press/Roli Books, 1996).

ANITA KHEMKA is a freelance photographer specialising in portraits of people on the edge. As well as

163

a photo story of the prostitutes of G.B. Road, Delhi, she has covered such diverse subjects as Bengali widows in Vrindavan, residents of mental asylums, eunuchs, child circus performers and *sadhus*, the Hindu religious ascetics. She was named one of the top 100 international photographers in the Golden Lights Awards (Maine, USA) in 1998.

FAWZAN HUSAIN has been photographing the sex workers of India since 1996. His photographic essay of the children of Kamathipura was acclaimed at his solo exhibitions in Baroda and Mumbai in 1997, and he has continued his expedition into the hearts of sex workers in his recent photography of Indian *hijras*. He has photographed for *Asiaweek* and *Mid-day* Publications and is presently a photo correspondent for *India Today*.

ANIS HAMDANI has photographed the lives of urban and rural people of his native Pakistan for many years. Now Chief Photographer for the *Daily Leader*, Karachi, Anis is also Pakistan photo correspondent for *Asiaweek*, *India Today* and Gamma Liaison photo news agency in New York.

ACHINTO has documented the lives of India's marginalised people since 1984. His work for NGOs and international agencies includes photographic studies of the lives, labour and habitats of Calcutta's poor, bonded labourers and child workers in the carpet industry of Uttar Pradesh, tribals in Orissa, and the fisherwomen of coastal West Bengal. His photographs have appeared in leading periodicals in India, Norway and the UK.

The Writers

JOHN FREDERICK is an advocacy writer and consultant to international organisations on gender and children's issues in South and Southeast Asia, particularly prostitution, trafficking, bonded labour and sexual abuse. He is the author of *Hopes For Tomorrow: The Children and Women of Nepal*, and *In Harm's Way: The Commercial Sexual Exploitation of South Asian Children*, among other publications. His articles on prostitution have appeared in many magazines and journals, and he was advisor to a nation-wide study of child prostitution and trafficking in Nepal for Unicef. His work with prostitution began 20 years ago as a social outreach worker with juvenile felons, including teenage sex workers. In the USA, he was Hawaii State Director of Women in Community Service, a social service

organisation for the rehabilitation of disadvantaged girls.

THÉRÈSE BLANCHET is an anthropologist who has been living and carrying out research in Bangladesh for the last 21 years. Her research on brothel prostitution started in 1993. She is the author of *Lost Innocence, Stolen Childhoods* (University Press Ltd., Dhaka, 1996), among other works.

ABHA DAYAL is a social activist, writer and the director/producer of more than 80 films and television productions, primarily on Indian children's and women's issues. She has directed and produced the film *Daughters of Darkness*, on the lives of child prostitutes in India.

V. CARROLL DUNHAM, an anthropologist by training, is the author of *The Hidden Himalayas* and co-author of *Tibet: Reflections from the Wheel of Life* (both

Abbeville Press). She has written extensively on prostitution, polyandry, abortion and birthlore in South Asia for international journals.

ANUSHEH HUSSAIN is the Director of Sahil, the only NGO in Pakistan which focuses solely on the issue of child sexual abuse. Anusheh has initiated counselling and referral programmes for abused children and conducted Pakistan's first major study on male child sex work.

HARSH MANDER's position as Director in the Department of Scheduled Caste Welfare of the Indian Administrative Service put him in intimate contact with the Bedia and Banjara communities. An activist, researcher and freelance writer, Harsh has written on sex work in his book *An Agenda for Caring* (Vikas, 1996).

RAJENDAR MENEN has written over 2,000 articles for more than 30 journals in five countries, including 100 articles on HIV/AIDS and related issues. He is the Executive Editor of *AIDS Update*, Mumbai, and has recently co-authored a book entitled *Positive Voices: Face To Face With HIV/AIDS*.

SUNIL MENON, social worker and anthropologist, is Project Co-ordinator of Sahodaran, a Chennai-based NGO working with male sexual health. He has conducted ethnographic research on males who have sex with males (MSMs) in Chennai, and has extensive experience as an outreach worker among *alis* and male sex workers.

CLIFF MEYERS is an educationist specialising in non-formal education, and is presently Chief of the Education Section of the Unicef Nepal Country Office. He co-ordinates and develops formal and non-formal basic education programmes for socially disadvantaged groups, including the Badi.

HASAN MUJTABA is a freelance writer for *Newsline* (Karachi), *Himal* (Kathmandu), BBC and Sindhi Media. His work on boy prostitution and on *hijras* has been published in the book *Islamic Homosexualities: Culture, History and Literature* (NYU Press, 1997).

LINNET PIKE has been conducting research since 1995 on issues related to the discourses on sex work in the Nepali context. A doctoral candidate in medical anthropology at the University of Queensland, Australia, she has conducted field work among the Badi community of Western Nepal.

MUNNI SAHA is Senior Reporter for the *Daily Bhorer Kagoj* of Dhaka, Bangladesh, and writes a column for the weekly journal *Chaltipatra*. Munni specialises in issues of prostitution, child labour, acid burning and domestic violence, and has produced a series of reports on prostitution in Bangladesh, India and Pakistan.

JEREMY SEABROOK's extensive writings have appeared in *The Guardian*, *The New Internationalist* and *The New Statesman*, among others. He is the author of many books on Asian development, social justice, urbanisation and sexuality, and most recently, *Love in a Different Climate* (Verso Press, 1999), about male-male sexual relations in South Asia.

VIDHEA SHRESTHA, photo editor, writer, researcher and interviewer, began work on prostitution in Nepal and India in 1993. She has conducted research and interviews on the Badi community, the *devadasis*, Nepal/India trafficking and AIDS interventions in Sonagachi brothel district, Calcutta.

THE PROTECTORS

Association for Community Development
Ms Salima Sarwar, Director
11/41 Saharpara, Rajshahi 6100 Bangladesh
Tel: (880-781) 774-546, Fax: (880-781) 775-383
Email: rajacd@bdcom.com

Devadasi Rehabilitation Project
Field Office, Myrada (Devi) Ghataprabha
Dr Konin Building, Doopdai Road,
Ghataprabha 591-306, Dist. Belgaum, Karnataka, India
Tel: (0831) 87416, 87316
Myrada Headquarters
No. 2 Service Road, Domblur Layout,
Bangalore 560-071, India
Tel: (080) 554-3166, 557-2028.

Don Bosco Technical Centre
Fr Anthony H. Pinto S.D.B., Director
22 Don Bosco MW, Ettukala, Negombo, Sri Lanka
Tel: (94-31) 24343, 38937, Fax: (94-31) 38207
Email: dbten@slt.lk

Durbar Mahila Samanwaya Committee
Ms Malla Singh, Secretary
8/2 Bhawani Dutta Lane, Calcutta 700-073 India
Tel: (91-33) 241-6283, 241-6200, Fax: (91-33) 241-6283
Email: ship@cal.vsnl.net.in

General Welfare Pratisthan
Mr Mahesh Bhattarai, Director
PO Box 3245, Kathmandu, Nepal
Tel: (977-1) 439-570, 422-935, Fax: (977-1) 417-979
Email: gwp@wlink.com.np

Halting AIDS on the Highways
Baruka Public Welfare Trust
Ms Asha Rao, Director, Mr Atanu Mazumdar
63 Rati Ahmed Kidwai Rd., Calcutta 700-016 India
Tel: (91-33) 244-9619, 245-8341, Fax: (91-33) 226-1196
Email: bpwt@cal.vsnl.net.in

Maiti Nepal
Ms Anuradha Koirala, Ms Armina Lama
P.O. Box 9599, Gaushala, Kathmandu, Nepal
Tel: (977-1) 475-316 Fax: (977-1) 253-993
Email: maiti@ccsl.com.np, maitinepal@wlink.com.np

Mukti Dhara Sansthan
Mr Ratan Katyayani
Mukti Ashram, Viratpur 303-102
Jaipur, Rajasthan, India

Naz Foundation (India) Trust
Ms Anjali Gopalan, Executive Director
3910 Andrews Gunj, New Delhi 110-049 India
Tel: (91-11) 656-7049, 656-3929
Fax: (91-11) 685-1970, Email: anjali@naz.unv.ernet.in

Sahil
(an important NGO working with child sexual abuse)
Ms Anusheh Hussain, Director
House 3, Street 32, Sector F-8/1, Islamabad, Pakistan
Tel: (92-51) 260-636, Fax: (92-51) 254-678
Email: ahussain@isb.comsats.net.pk
Website: www.sahil.org

Social Awareness for Education
Mr Dilip Pariyar, President
Fultekra Line, Ward #7, Nepalgunj, Nepal
Tel: (977-81) 21449, Fax: (977-81) 21618
Email: safe@vishnu.ccsl.com.np

STD/HIV Intervention Programme
Dr Smarajit Jana
8/2 Bhawani Dutta Lane, Calcutta 700-073 India
Tel: (91-33) 241-6283, 241-6200, Fax: (91-33) 241-6283
Email: ship@cal.vsnl.net.in

BIBLIOGRAPHY

Banerjee, Sumanta. *Dangerous Outcaste: The Prostitute in Nineteenth Century Bengal*. Calcutta: Seagull, 1998.

Bell, Laurie, ed. *Good Girls/Bad Girls: Feminists and Sex Trade Workers Talk Face to Face*. Toronto: The Women's Press, 1987.

Blanchet, Thérèse. *Children in Brothels* (Draft Report). Child Study Series. Dhaka: Rädda Barnen, 1994.

D'Cunha, Jean. *The Legalisation of Prostitution: A Sociological Inquiry into the Laws Relating to Prostitution in India and the West*. (A Joint Women's Programme publication). New Delhi: Uppal Publishing House, 1991.

Delacoste, Frederique and Priscilla Alexander, eds. *Sex Work: Writings by Women in the Sex Industry*. London: Virago Press, 1993.

International Committee for Prostitutes' Rights. *World Charter for Prostitutes' Rights*. Amsterdam: ICPR, 1998.

Jayawardene, K. and M. de Alwis, eds. *Embodied Violence: Communalizing Women's Sexuality in South Asia*. New Delhi: Kali for Women, 1996.

Joarder, B. *Prostitution in Modern and Historical Perspectives*. New Delhi: Inter India, 1984.

Khan, Zarina Rahman and H.K. Arefeen. *Potita Nari: A Study of Prostitution in Bangladesh*. Dhaka: Centre for Social Studies, 1989.

Murray, Stephan O., ed. *Islamic Homosexualities: Culture History and Literature*. New York: New York University Press, 1997.

Nanda, Serena. *Neither Man nor Woman: The Hijras of India*. Belmont, CA: Wadsworth Publishing House, 1990.

Naz Foundation ki Pukaar (Newsletter of the Naz Foundation). London, New Delhi: Shivlok Enterprises.

Pheterson, Gail, ed. *A Vindication of the Rights of Whores*. Seattle: Seal Press, 1989.

Pike, L. (in press). "Sex Work and Socialisation in a Moral World: Change and Conflict in Badi Communities of West Nepal." In L. Manderson and P. Liamputtong Rice, eds. *Coming of Age: Youth, Courtship and Sexuality in South and Southeast Asia*.

Roberts, Nickie. *Whores in History: Prostitution in Western Society*. London: Harper-Collins, 1992.

Rozario, Sr. R. M. *Trafficking in Women and Children in India*. (A Joint Women's Programme publication). New Delhi: Uppal Publishing House, 1988.

Sangari, Kum Kum and Sudesh Vaid, eds. *Recasting Women: Essays in Colonial History*. New Delhi: Kali for Women, 1993.

Sanghera, Jyoti. "Trafficking and Prostitution in South Asia from a Third World Perspective." In Hugh Johnston and Sona Khan, eds. *Trafficking in Persons in South Asia*. Calgary: Shastri Indo-Canadian Institute, 1998.

Seabrook, Jeremy. *Love in a Different Climate*. London: Verso Press, 1999.

Sleighthome, C. and I. Sinha. *Guilty Without Trial: Women in the Sex Trade in Calcutta*. Calcutta: Stree, 1996.

Page 168: A brothel afternoon. A woman looks down on the street, waiting for clients. *Kamathipura, Mumbai.*
Shehzad Noorani

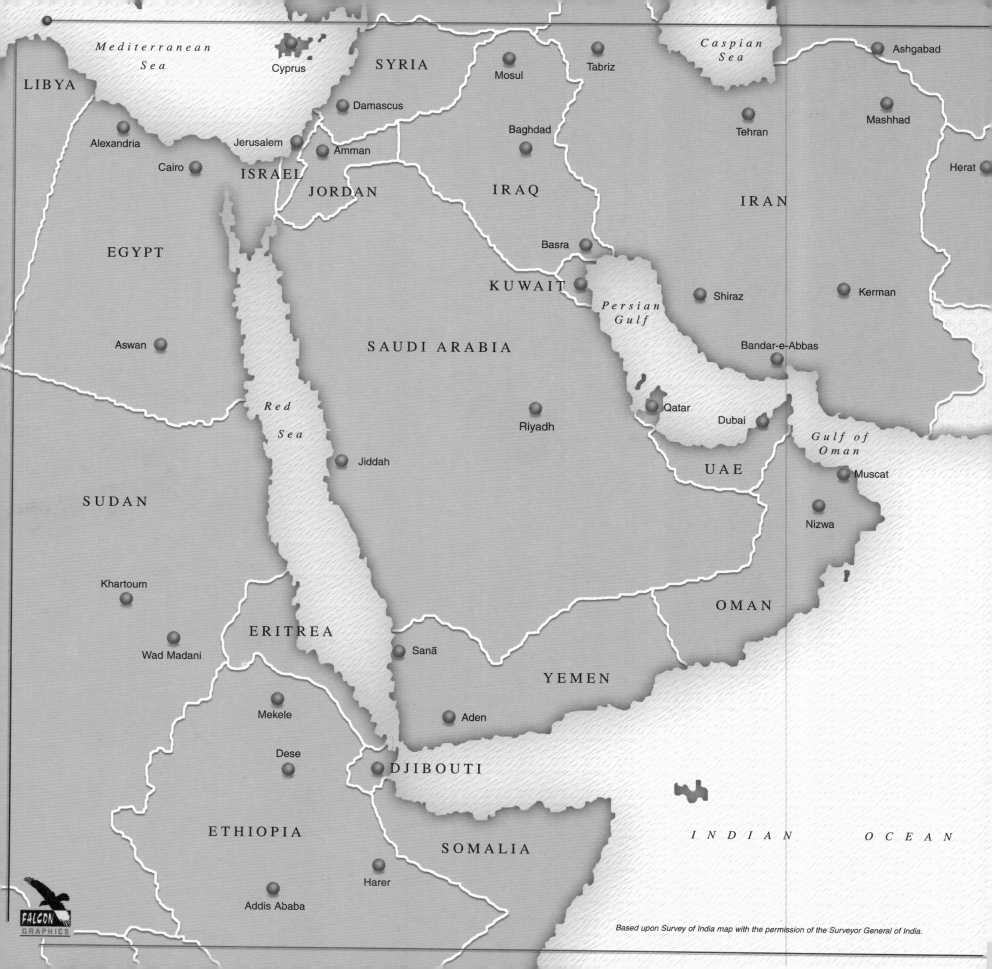

LIBYA

Mediterranean Sea

Cyprus

SYRIA

Damascus

Jerusalem

Amman

ISRAEL

JORDAN

Alexandria

Cairo

EGYPT

Aswan

Red Sea

Jiddah

SUDAN

Khartoum

Wad Madani

ERITREA

Mekele

Dese

ETHIOPIA

Addis Ababa

Harer

DJIBOUTI

SOMALIA

Mosul

Tabriz

Baghdad

IRAQ

Basra

KUWAIT

Persian Gulf

SAUDI ARABIA

Riyadh

Qatar

UAE

Dubai

Sanā

YEMEN

Aden

Caspian Sea

Ashgabad

Tehran

Mashhad

Herat

IRAN

Shiraz

Kerman

Bandar-e-Abbas

Gulf of Oman

Muscat

Nizwa

OMAN

INDIAN OCEAN

Based upon Survey of India map with the permission of the Surveyor General of India.

FALCON
GRAPHICS